PARALEGAL LITIGATION AND PRACTICE LIBRARY FROM WILEY LAW PUBLICATIONS

D1556597

SUBSCRIPTION NOTICE

HOW TO SURVIVE IN A LAW FIRM: Client Relations

By Nancy Pulsifer
Dana L. Graves
&
Jill S. Levin, Esq.

Wiley Law Publications
JOHN WILEY & SONS, INC.
New York • Chichester • Brisbane • Toronto • Singapore

Preface

As editor of the Paralegal Library for Wiley Law Publications, it is my pleasure to introduce the first in a series of books published in cooperation with Estrin Publishing. Both Wiley Law Publications and Estrin Publishing share a commitment to excellence in this product, and a desire to provide legal professionals with useful, practice-oriented material. This "survival series" is designed to equip both lawyers and legal assistants with the skills necessary to handle the complex problems they will face in the law firm, and to expand both professional and personal horizons.

The first three topics in this series deal with interpersonal communications, billing techniques and ethics. What do these issues have to do with client relations? Whether you are a novice or seasoned professional, if you have worked during at least one monthly billing cycle at a law firm, I believe you know the answer.

Billing for legal services is an extremely sensitive issue with clients, and one that can be very ambiguous. Unlike medicine, the benefits of legal services are not always readily apparent. The only thing that is obvious, especially in protracted litigation, is that the client must usually continue to pay before a final result is determined. The benefits of working and billing efficiently are passed onto the client in reduced fees. Proper time descriptions provide clients with a sense that they are getting the most for their money. There is nothing more vexing than to have to answer billing questions each month, and not have the proper documentation necessary to back up the expense. With the sample forms and detailed explanations contained in *Counting the Minutes*, Dana L. Graves shows the benefits of organization and efficiency on increased productivity and client satisfaction.

Ethics is an issue addressed in the remarkably complete and concise *This Business of Confidentiality: What Everyone Doesn't Need to Know.* Jill S. Levin and Dana L. Graves explain the standards of ethics and how they are applied in a real world context. Most legal issues are very private and personal to the principals involved, and there are a great many ways that confidences can be inadvertently breached. The authors offer practical advice on how to tighten security and institute systems which will assure the client that matters are kept within the confines of the firm.

There may be no other issue affecting a client that is more important than learning to work with the attorney. If there is difficulty in communicating your questions or needs on a case, or if assignments are misunderstood, the end result will be a poor work product. The firm may lose a case because of ineffective communication, and be subjected to the ire of the client. In *Unwritten Rules*, Nancy Pulsifer presents tips on handling tasks from initial assignment through disposition of the particular matter. Along the way, the author gives valuable insights into working with other staff, setting up checklists and how to organize your workload effectively. This is an issue that is absolutely vital to increasing the positive benefits that legal professionals can provide to clients.

I know you will find these discussions useful, and would hope that you continue to develop and expand the skills which the authors present so masterfully. I would like to thank them for their commitment to the profession, and their dedication to this project. I would also like to thank Chere B. Estrin and Dana L. Graves of Estrin Publishing, and Mark Helland of Wiley Law Publications. It is through their vision and efforts that this series is possible.

November 1992

Mike Vetrano, Editor
Wiley Law Publications

Summary Contents

Detailed Contents

PART I UNWRITTEN RULES:

A Guide to Successfully Working with Attorneys

Chapter 1. Taking an Assignment   1

Chapter 2. Identifying the Lawyer's Expectations   15

Chapter 5. While Working on the Assignment 59

Chapter 6. When You Return the Assignment   85

Chapter 7. After the Project Is Done   91

Index   A-1

PART II   COUNTING THE MINUTES:

The Essential Training Guide for Time & Billing Techniques

Chapter 4. General Policy Issues Affecting Time Billing 23

Chapter 5. The Mechanics of Timekeeping 37

Chapter 6. Ensuring Time Billed Is Actually Charged to the Client 49

Chapter 7. Time Management Tools   59

Chapter 8. Time Billing Management Reports   67

Chapter 9. Minimum Annual Billable Hours Requirements   77

PART III   THIS BUSINESS OF CONFIDENTIALITY:

What Everyone <u>Doesn't</u> Need to Know

Chapter 4. Conflict of Interest   43

Chapter 5. Common Sense Tips for Protecting Confidential Information   57

UNWRITTEN RULES

A Guide to Successfully Working with Attorneys

by Nancy Pulsifer

Foreword by John G. Ferreira
Reed Smith Shaw & McClay

Publisher's Note

Unwritten Rules contains suggestions to help you deal and work effectively with lawyers. It is not meant to replace any policy, procedures or any other guidelines your firm may have. Be sure to review your firm's employee handbook, if any, and check with all appropriate personnel for specific guidance concerning your firm's expectations.

The author welcomes comments and suggestions from readers. Address any letters to the Publisher.

Foreword

Like many of my generation, I was a "Trekkie" in my teens. One of my favorite "Star Trek" episodes is the one in which Captain Kirk confounds the villains by tricking them into playing an imaginary card game called "Fizzbin."

The gambit is that Kirk simply makes up the game as he goes along, never telling the villains all the rules, and changing the rules as soon as the villains think they understand them: "Well, ordinarily two queens **would** beat a red seven, but not on Tuesdays."

The first day on the job at a law firm feels a lot like being dragged into a game of "Fizzbin." You are immediately thrust into a world full of hazy, unwritten and unspoken rules and expectations, and you are expected to figure them out largely on your own, quickly, and without bothering anybody with too many questions.

The academic experience—that cocoon-like atmosphere, where all the problems are hypothetical, and time and talk is free—is far removed from the realities of law practice. Leaving that world and arriving, with little preparation, at the rough and tumble of a law practice is a massive jolt—one from which some newcomers never recover.

Think of the pages that follow as your secret weapon in the fight to survive, and thrive, in a law firm: your personal guide to those unwritten and unspoken rules and expectations. Nancy Pulsifer has spent over 17 years working successfully with as unruly and demanding a bunch of lawyers as exist in any law practice anywhere (trust me on this one). She has kept a detailed record of all the tricks of the trade—all the things that lawyers expect, and demand (reasonable and otherwise) from the professionals who work for them. And, for your benefit, she has written them down, in a straightforward, lucid text. What follows, simply, is the best guide for new lawyers, and legal assistants, that I have ever read.

John G. Ferreira
Reed Smith Shaw & McClay

Acknowledgements

I would like to thank Pamela J. Bailey, CLAS, for her long-standing conviction that this text is necessary for paralegals and lawyers, and for her encouragement to get it published. I also wish to thank Beth L. Silver, Esq., for her support and her substantial editing assistance. Finally, I want to thank the law firm of Reed Smith Shaw & McClay for providing the experiences upon which to base this text and for the resources to write it, particularly "bert."

My thanks also to John G. Ferreira for developing and teaching me the seven key questions to ask about assignments as well as the concept of active listening.

Introduction

In most law firms and corporate law departments, it can take one or two years for new paralegals and associates to develop the skills and work habits that will enable them to work effectively with lawyers. Often, these skills are learned only by trial and error, because the "unwritten rules" for success are not the kind that can be conveyed during orientation.

This monograph tells you all the unwritten rules. It shows you how to work successfully with very busy and demanding lawyers. It tells you what you need to do when a lawyer gives you an assignment: how to take notes, what to ask, and how to determine the lawyer's expectations. It gives you a thorough checklist of the working procedures that most lawyers assume others know intuitively. It also tells you how to develop the kind of work habits that lawyers take for granted.

The Problem

School does not always prepare you for the working world. Success in school and knowledge of the law are only part of what you need to know to succeed in the legal world. There are many new skills you will need that no one has (or ever intends) to teach you. Lawyers have many assumptions and expectations that you must identify and fulfill. Moreover, the standards by which you will be judged are different than those you were trained to expect in school.

Even with the most sophisticated of orientation programs (for which law firms are not known), much is left unsaid. The problem is that the whole bundle of rules and expectations is just too complicated to go through in the amount of time most lawyers have for training. And even if lawyers and paralegal managers did have the time, they may not have identified all those expectations in a comprehensive or systematic way. To the extent that you are provided any training beyond the substance of the practice, it will most likely focus on teaching you to avoid the specific mistakes that your teachers or your predecessors have made, without identifying the overall work habits that lawyers require.

Most of the procedures discussed in this monograph appear to be common sense once you identify them; certainly they are to lawyers. They are not common sense, however, to most people when they begin to work in a law office.

How *Unwritten Rules* Helps

When you work for a lawyer, your job is to save the lawyer time. To do this, you need to accomplish all assignments accurately and efficiently, keeping client costs in mind. The skills and procedures you use to achieve those goals are many and detailed. How quickly you grasp the rules, how fast you work, how many mistakes you make, how well you work with others, and what impression you give in the process, comprise the standards by which you will be judged. This monograph gives you a definite advantage in meeting those goals, and as a result, provides you with all the secrets for a successful career.

How *Unwritten Rules* Is Organized

Unwritten Rules is about the process of receiving and completing assignments for lawyers. It does not deal with the law or the substance of the work that paralegals or lawyers perform.

This monograph is organized in approximately the order in which you will receive and complete an assignment for a lawyer. It starts at the point where you are first given an assignment and must identify the lawyer's expectations. Next, it lists steps you should take before you begin the assignment. It then discusses how to work with people on assignments: dealing with lawyers, your secretary and clients. A section on how to organize yourself and your work load follows.

Finally, you'll find a discussion about how to return the assignment to the lawyer and determine any follow-up requirements.

Unwritten Rules will remind you of tasks as mundane as dating your notes, and as complex as how to organize yourself and communicate effectively. It offers tips for handling interruptions and the pitfalls of using computers. It also illustrates the consequences of failing to follow these guidelines.

Where *Unwritten Rules* Came From and Why

Since lawyers and law firms rarely identify their expectations or take the time to teach good work habits to their employees, I started keeping a list of the misconceptions and errors that I encountered (or made myself). Thus, this is a detailed list of practical rules, tips and hints that are factual because they are compiled from actual work experiences.

I happen to work in the area of employee benefits, and therefore you'll find some examples are drawn from that area. Even when other practice areas are illustrated, however, the strength of this monograph is that the guidance it contains comes from actual experiences.

The goal of *Unwritten Rules* is simple: you should not have to make mistakes to learn from them.

1

Taking an Assignment

In the field of law, how you complete an assignment—whether it is accurate, on time and cost-effective, as well as whether you are asked to do the same type of assignment again—can be directly affected by how well you and your supervising lawyers communicate.

BASICS TO REMEMBER

Because **you** are ultimately responsible for the results of your assignment, you must get precisely the right directions in the very first meeting with the lawyer. Before you begin an assignment, you need the answers to seven key questions:

1) What are the legal issues? Note any issues that you should **not** look at.

2) In what form should the work product be? For example, does the lawyer need a letter, memo, brief, oral response, or copies of cases? What does the lawyer expect back from you?

3) When does the lawyer need it? Also, are there any real (i.e., statutory or court-imposed) deadlines?

4) To what client (and what matter) should your time be charged?

5) How many hours are you expected to spend on the project?

6) Where would the lawyer look if this assignment was not delegated? Where would the lawyer begin?

7) If you are drafting a document, does the lawyer have a form or sample to follow?

The **procedural** aspects of these questions are the subject of this chapter and the next.

TIME FRAMES AND DEADLINES

One of the most crucial details of any assignment is the due date. You must find out both the "hard" deadlines and the "soft" ones:

- Are there any statutory, regulatory, court-imposed, or other external deadlines?

- Are there any client-imposed deadlines or expectations?

- When does the lawyer want the assignment to be completed, and how long should it take?

Discuss with the lawyer any other projects you have that might delay your beginning to work on this new assignment. Be sure to tell the lawyer when you can start working, and when you expect to finish the assignment.

TIME BUDGETS

Find out the guidelines for the amount of time to be billed to the client. Is there a time budget or an hours limit you cannot exceed? If so, that will tell you a great deal about the scope of the assignment.

You may estimate that the project will take at least two days. However, if the lawyer expects only two hours to be billed to the client, either you have misunderstood the project, or the lawyer may not be aware of what will be involved to complete it. Resolve this question **before** you spend the time, not after.

CHARGING YOUR TIME

Think of the time spent doing legal work for a client as the "product" which a law firm "manufactures." Lawyers are usually not paid by the project for completed wills, briefs or pension plans; they are paid for the time spent on these projects. But a law firm can only be paid for those hours which it bills to clients. And a law firm can only bill clients for those hours which are properly recorded by the person doing the work.

Thus, most lawyers and paralegals must keep records, known as "time sheets" or "logs," on which they record the amount of time which is to be charged or billed to clients, along with detailed descriptions of the work performed. Usually these are handwritten records which are then translated by secretaries into the firm's computer system for billing clients. The billing statement sent to a client may reflect more or less detail concerning the work performed, depending upon the arrangement and relationship which the firm has with that client. (Advice concerning exactly how to record billable time appears in **Chapter 5**, under the heading, "Record Your Time.")

To accurately record your time, you must obtain from the lawyer the name of the client that should be billed at the beginning of the assignment. Many clients have different "matters" which may be used to designate separate types of legal work (different cases or deals) being done for the same client. You (and your secretary) must be sure to record your time properly. (If you have not already received orientation regarding billing in your firm or department, now is the time.)

Lawyers and paralegals must record the following information, usually on a daily basis:

- the client's name (often there is a client number assigned by the firm);

- the specific client matter which differentiates your work from other projects being worked on for that client (and may also identify the type of work being done, such as corporate deals, a case being litigated, real estate closings, a tax return or a labor arbitration). Again, your firm may assign specific numbers to each individual client matter;

- a description of the work performed (*see* the discussion in **Chapter 5** detailing how to write appropriate time descriptions);

- the number of hours and fractions of hours spent, according to the firm's system (some firms bill in quarter-hour increments, some in tenths of hours);

- sometimes it is important to include the name of the lawyer who assigned the work; this can be particularly true for paralegals, and if the assignment is of short duration.

While the identity of the client and the matter on which you'll be working may be obvious from the documents or file you are given, you will also find situations when this information is not apparent. For example, a lawyer may ask you for a copy of a case or for sample documents. If you do not know the name of the client for whom these items are needed, a simple "And who's this for?" before the lawyer gets away down the hall will do it. Your secretary can obtain the appropriate billing numbers later.

During the initial assignment conference, the client and matter numbers are important pieces of the background information to be conveyed, and if the lawyer does not mention this, you should. Correcting erroneous time charges later is tedious, not usually considered billable time, and may even be embarrassing. Therefore, do not leave this critical detail out.

NONBILLABLE TIME

Generally, all working time must be accounted for on your time records, even if the work performed is not for a client. For example, you may be required to work on firm activities such as client development, legal work for the firm or office administrative tasks. Paralegals often index and update sample files and form documents, case summaries and numerous other resources specific to their practice areas. Attorneys and paralegals alike may be involved in civic activities such as charitable or pro bono work.

Your firm may have a list of "office numbers" or "administrative codes" to which nonbillable projects are charged. You may be required to obtain authorization to charge time to such numbers. Or, you may be given a "nonbillable time budget" setting forth the maximum amount of time the firm expects you to charge to such activities.

Find out how your firm handles these nonbillable matters and how your firm views such work. Nonbillable time may be an integral and valued part of your work at the firm. However, because it may not generate immediate revenues for the firm, nonbillable projects are often valued less highly than billable work. In any event, accurate recording of time spent is as critical for nonbillable time as it is for client-related matters.

HAVE A POSITIVE ATTITUDE

Approach every new assignment cheerfully and willingly, keeping in mind two possible reservations. You should always disclose your inexperience when asked to take on a new type of project for the first time (*see* more on this point below). And if you simply cannot take on any additional work because of prior commitments, you should so advise the attorney.

Yes, there will always be projects that neither you nor anyone else really wants. But always be conscious of your expression and attitude as you are approached for new assignments.

Unbelievable as this may seem, in the long run, that first 30-second impression can outweigh even how fast or how well you actually do the assignment. As mentioned, this does **not** mean you pretend you know how to do everything. But a willingness to accept assignments, no matter what the level of challenge, will convey that you are receptive to new and different assignments. If lawyers feel free to give you work, you will naturally get more work, and gain more experience, variety and professional growth.

The impression of a positive attitude is an amazingly influential determinant of who will give you work and how much you will receive. It is much easier to give new projects to someone who is willing to tackle them. Once you've developed the reputation as a professional who can handle those challenging and therefore more exciting projects, the more mundane tasks will be assigned less and less frequently. Keep the following phrase in mind and use it often: "No problem."

DISCLOSE YOUR INEXPERIENCE

It is **always** a good idea to disclose your inexperience about an assignment at the time it is given. You do not want lawyers to assume that you are well versed in an area if you are not. Of course, you should at the same time express your confidence in being able to learn how to handle the project. However, if you have not done an assignment before, every aspect of the project may take more time:

■ the assignment will need to be explained more carefully;

■ you may have more questions and unexpected problems than ordinarily would be the case;

■ it may take you more time than usual to complete the assignment;

■ your progress will need to be supervised more closely;

■ your finished assignment will need to be reviewed more carefully.

The lawyer needs to know about your inexperience in cases where there are strict time deadlines, client charges must be kept to a minimum, or when the lawyer simply does not have the additional time necessary to work with you through your inexperience.

KEEP YOUR WORK AT AN APPROPRIATE LEVEL

Occasionally, you will be asked to handle tasks that are ordinarily clerical in nature, such as copying. These kinds of assignments may be given to associates as well as paralegals. Because this can happen in a number of situations, you will need to differentiate them in order to operate at a cost-effective level.

You may be handed clerical work just because you are the closest person. Lawyers often assume that giving clerical work to anyone who is billed at a lower rate than they are is cost effective, and that may be true, to an extent. It is indeed more cost effective for you to find the secretary to handle the work than it is for a senior attorney to do so. This does **not** mean, however, that you must handle the clerical work yourself. It just means you have to make sure that it gets done.

Give the assignment to your secretary, mail room or copy center, whichever is appropriate. Instruct your secretary (mailroom or copy clerk) that this work is to be done as soon as possible and that it should be returned directly to the lawyer.

Remember there will be times when everyone is expected — and needed — to pitch in just to get the job done. For example, you may be on a team scrambling to make last minute changes in multitudes of documents to reflect the ever-changing terms of a deal. If that means that partners need to copy documents, associates prepare Federal Express packages and paralegals type labels, then these jobs must be done. Pitching in to do whatever is necessary **will** be noticed.

In additional rare circumstances, there might be a need for you, and not a secretary, to handle a particular clerical job. Confidentiality may be a factor, although as a practical matter, secretaries are included in the vast majority of projects that would be ordinarily be considered confidential. An exception might be the firm's own business.

If the lawyer's purpose in giving you clerical work is not clear from the outset, ask which client should be billed for your work on this project. This can result in redirection of the task to a secretary. Or, if the lawyer really does require a paralegal or associate to handle this work, you are alerting the lawyer to the fact that the client will be billed for your time.

Be aware that lawyers (and your firm) really do expect you to be operating at the most cost-effective level. It is up to you to make sure you are doing so.

> **Specific Advice for Paralegals:** The occasions when lawyers ask paralegals to perform tasks more appropriate to support staff can unfortunately occur fairly often. If you do not conscientiously avoid clerical work, you may sooner or later find yourself doing it.

> Because paralegals have billable hour requirements just like associates, it is your responsibility to ensure that your time is used appropriately. Fortunately, with diligence, and awareness of the problem, this **can** be accomplished. For example, when asked by a new secretary how the copiers work, introduce him or her to someone else who can help and does not have billable hours requirements.

> Paralegals are not hired at law firms simply to fill in the gaps anymore, but to generate billable—and that means collectable—hours for the firm.

ALWAYS TAKE NOTES

Taking comprehensive notes during assignment meetings is important. At the outset of a new project, the most relevant or important facts may not be easily apparent. You might not know enough about the subject matter yet to perfectly understand the issues. And you don't want to be in the position of realizing later, for example, that whether the sale is a stock sale or an asset sale is a very important factor, when all you've written down is "sale."

During the initial meeting in which you are given an assignment, you should record a detailed account of everything the lawyer says, including the following:

- the issues in the case;

- the background and history of the case;

- what the firm expects to accomplish and how;

- who the responsible parties are.

You should also:

- pay particular attention to getting the facts straight;

- find out whether the facts need to be verified;

- find out who has the case files and pertinent documents; and

- keep a separate list of the tasks you are to perform, and the order in which they should be completed.

This last item is the most important. **Always** read the list of tasks back to the lawyer to make sure you both understand what projects you will be handling and when. Refer back to your notes periodically to make sure you are staying on track and picking up all the necessary elements of the assignment. Review your notes again at the end of the project as a double check. If you rely only on your memory, your finished product may come in wide of the mark because you have confused what the lawyer actually said with what occurred to you as the lawyer was talking and what occurred to you later, as work progressed on the assignment.

Additional, practical tips for note taking, and the reasons for their importance, follow.

- Date your meeting notes, and in fact, all notes of even chance conversations with the supervising attorney.

The date is a small fact that is easily recorded but often difficult to reconstruct later. You won't always know whether the date you recorded the notes may later prove helpful or necessary. For example, if the lawyer needs a breakdown of your time from the date you began working on the project, you can easily give your secretary this information if you've dated the initial meeting notes. Dating your notes can also remind you how long the project has been sitting on your desk. Get in the habit of always including the date.

- Make note of any terms of art and terms with which you're not familiar.

It's true that people often do not hear what they have not yet learned to recognize. Remember the example of learning a new word and then hearing it again twice in the next week? It was there all along—you just never recognized it before. The only way to guard against this is to write down **everything**.

- Record notes as neatly as possible; you may not have time to recopy them, and you must be able to read your own notes.

Particularly when the lawyer gives you an example of what he or she has in mind, try to capture as many of the details as you can. Some lawyers will talk as though they were dictating a memo, so you may be able to catch only the intended "flavor" of the example. But be sure to record at least the gist of the comments; some of these details may be what are expected in the finished project.

- Verify important facts.

Just because your notes reflect that a lawyer said something does **not** necessarily mean that it is gospel. For example, if the lawyer said "the sale occurred on October 20, 1990," do not assume that this is the correct date. Check the sales agreement to confirm that date. Better yet, while you are still in the assignment meeting, ask whether you need to verify the date of the sale. The objective is to be as accurate as possible without spending unnecessary time. When there is **any** question, however, always double-check.

There are times when statements can be misleading if you take them literally. For example, many people do not readily know which months have 30 days and which have 31. You may receive an instruction to "file it on the 30th of August." This instruction may really mean the last day of August, the day before the last day, or even the last business day of the month. When there are multiple possibilities, especially if common sense might indicate a more likely alternative, always ask to make sure.

BE CAREFUL WITH TERMS OF ART

Sometimes terms of art are used generically, or they may have different meanings in different situations. People also sometimes refer to complicated matters by using a shorthand term.

For example: You attend a meeting where a number of people refer to a single sum payment from a pension plan as a "lump sum distribution." That does not necessarily mean, however, that the distribution has met all the technical requirements for being a "lump sum distribution" under Internal Revenue Code § 402(e). Everyone in the meeting also may be calling this transaction a "merger of the pension plans," but for IRS purposes, a discontinuance of contributions to one of the pension plans may in fact be considered a termination. This means you have to file the long form for termination, **not** the short form for merger.

People working in specific practice areas often develop shorthand methods for referring to events, laws and transactions. You will need to either ask for an explanation or find a resource where these terms are explained. It may be that the terms used are peculiar to your firm or organization. In such cases, be certain you understand the terms before acting on them.

VOLUNTEER FOR RELATED WORK

In order to save time and footwork, ask at the beginning of a new project if there are any related assignments that you can attend to at the same time. Be on the lookout for related work and then volunteer to do it. Anticipating the lawyer's needs saves time, which lawyers value highly.

The related assignments that are relevant to your area of practice will become apparent as you work. For example, for a tax or pension issue, a special power of attorney may be required to deal with the Internal Revenue Service. Or, if your project is to find the names of expert witnesses, you may volunteer to find out when they last testified or to obtain their biographies. You can phrase your questions as follows:

- "After preparing the outline for the deposition, would you also like me to prepare the chronology of events?"

- "Before drafting the answers to interrogatories, do you need a summary of medical records?"

- "Do you want me to go ahead and prepare the Points and Authorities after finishing the research?"

Cover letters provide another good example of related assignments. Documents are rarely prepared without being sent somewhere, so a cover letter is almost always needed. Volunteer to draft the letter.

Be aware of one possible pitfall: After the initial assignment meeting, other aspects of the project may occur to you. Before you go ahead and work on those related tasks, however, ask if they are necessary (or even wanted). It may be that the client is on a strict budget, and billings must be kept to a minimum. Or, someone else may have already been assigned the related task. Perhaps the lawyer has simply not thought about it. By asking first, you will provide the attorney an opportunity to veto additional work, know that additional time will be billed, or offer advice on how to accomplish this particular task.

VOLUNTEER TO TAKE CARE OF LOOSE ENDS

With any project, there are loose ends to tie up. Just as with volunteering for related work, you can save the lawyer time if you take care of all the details that are necessary to complete a project. By taking care of the project from beginning to end, you can make yourself indispensable.

For example, ask if you should make sure that all the appropriate parties—such as accountants, other lawyers, deponents, trustees, escrow officers, expert witnesses and consultants, etc.—have copies of necessary documents. You can take care of reminders for the next phase of the project, setting up the next meeting, or making sure signed copies are obtained for the files. Sometimes taking care of the loose ends simply means checking to see that the support staff finishes its job correctly. Be sure, however, that if you volunteer to see that the final details are handled, you understand exactly what tasks remain to be done, and then follow through.

2

Identifying the Lawyer's Expectations

Conveying—and understanding—the lawyer's expectations for an assignment are the most difficult parts of the assignment process.

EXPECTATIONS

Realize that it is not always easy to accurately delegate an assignment. Cooperate by being an active listener. Do not just nod, take notes, and take everything at face value.

Find out **exactly** what the lawyer expects or needs from you for any particular project. Keep asking questions until you are sure you understand what the lawyer wants. Then double-check your understanding by reviewing the assignment points with the lawyer again. If the lawyer appears impatient with additional questions, remember that he or she will surely be more upset if the end result is incorrect.

SCOPE

Ask the lawyer to define the scope of your assignment. For example, if the attorney mentions a number of details for you to handle, find out whether she wants you to do just those specifically, or whether she expects you to review and be responsible for everything else as well.

As noted above, if you are unsure about whether you should handle a peripheral part of the assignment that looks necessary, ask before you do it. Someone else may be doing that part of the assignment or it may be unnecessary. It is better to ask, even if it means interrupting the lawyer, than to charge time which later must be written off. (Time is considered "written off" if it is deleted from the bill before it is sent to the client.)

FORMAT

If the lawyer gives you a question to resolve or a research assignment, determine in what form you should provide the answer. For example, does the lawyer want a formal memo in the standard Question/Issue, Answer, Facts and Discussion format? Or does the attorney just want the underlying documents with the appropriate pages clipped, along with a handwritten outline or summary of your results?

Find out how the answer will be used: Does the lawyer need to write a letter to the client or simply make a phone call? If the end result will be a letter, perhaps you can tailor your memo so that parts of it can be inserted directly into the letter. If the answer is required for a telephone call, maybe all that is needed is a note with the answer and the client's name and phone number.

THOROUGHNESS (ACCURACY) vs. SPEED

Be aware of the trade-off between these two conflicting interests: thoroughness (or accuracy) and speed. Determine how critical the accuracy is, while at the same time keeping in mind the client's ability and/or willingness to pay. In some cases, a job done in two hours with 90% accuracy is preferable to a job done in five hours with 99% accuracy (or a job done in nine hours with 100% accuracy), if the ultimate goal is a quick and inexpensive project.

Try to get a feel for which side to err on with each lawyer and each project. Unfortunately, you will usually find that most attorneys want the project done in one hour with 100% accuracy.

COMPREHENSIVE vs. EDITED

Would the lawyer rather have you include every possible angle, so that all he or she must do is delete unneeded information or text? Or should you make the editing choices, while noting which areas could be expanded?

With the second approach, you take a shorter, less costly route initially, but you let the lawyer know what information you have excluded. You have also noted other areas for consideration and indicated that you are prepared to spend more time to make additions if necessary. The goal is to save the lawyer time, while accomplishing the project with the lowest overall cost to the client.

USING SAMPLES AND FORM FILES

Using existing sample documents can help you finish a project more quickly, provide a great catalyst for your own thinking, and give you a double check on your work. Not using good, available samples is inefficient. However, guard against using them as a crutch.

Do **not** allow the availability of others' work to become a substitute for working through problems yourself. Compromise by using the best of what others have done before, combined with the best of what you have to contribute, to make the final product better. This may require rethinking the problem from scratch before you ever look at, and thus become fixed on, someone else's format or language.

On the other hand, if the lawyer gives you a sample to use, **follow that sample**. Do not rewrite it into a style that suits you. When in doubt, ask: "Do you want me to follow this as closely as possible or is this just somewhere for me to begin?"

One problem with using samples is that they are often tailored to a particular fact or legal situation which may not be the same as yours. You may have to go back to the law or regulations to see what was required in the first place in order to find out whether the sample document the lawyer gave you includes all the elements necessary in your case. It is usually easy to see what parts of the sample do not apply to your situation; it's much harder to see what information was left out that you might need to add.

For instance, the sample Internal Revenue Code tax notice you find in the form files might not apply to your pension plan because the plan the notice was drafted for did not have the following elements: deductible employee contributions, contributions before 1974, self-employed persons or beneficiaries other than surviving spouses, while yours does. Look at the law behind the sample language and not just at the sample in order to keep from missing important elements.

3

Before You Begin Working

Before you start a project, it's always a good idea to acquaint yourself with the files, sample documents and the procedures necessary for completing the assignment.

DEADLINES AGAIN—BOTH PRACTICAL AND REAL

Determine the deadlines again for yourself **before you do anything else**. Even if you think you know the deadline, take a second and very careful look.

Then, consider all the possible roadblocks: will the client need to sign the final document before the deadline and might the key signatory be on vacation? Allow for the time it will take the secretaries to type the necessary papers, and for the lawyer and the client to review and comment on the draft documents. You may find you have less time than you think.

You need to establish these practical deadlines so you can plan your own time. Do you work on this now or next week? If you don't account for all the required elements until you look at the project next week, you may find that you haven't budgeted sufficient time. Remember Murphy's Law: you can almost guarantee that when you pick up the assignment next week, you will discover that the person who needs to sign the form will not be back until after the deadline, or that you have just missed the last Board of Directors meeting for the year.

It is surprising how many crises can be avoided (at least temporarily) by a closer look at the **apparent** deadline. For example, you may find that, because of an exception in the law that applies to your client, or because of the facts particular to your client, you have more or less time than you originally thought to complete the work. Or, you could determine that because the deadline falls on a Saturday, you have an additional day to finish the project.

Remember, the person assigning the project may not always be on top of this degree of detail. The attorney may have a general deadline in mind, but on closer look, you find that the specific deadline applicable in your case is different. In such cases, you must inform the lawyer as soon as possible.

Because you have been assigned the project, it is up to you to take that closer look at both the practical **and** real deadlines.

BUDGET YOUR TIME AND WORK EFFICIENTLY

Estimate for yourself how long the assignment should realistically take, and don't allow yourself to spend more time than that. As you gain experience, it is important to keep reducing the time it takes to complete the same (or similar) projects. With your growing experience, lawyers will also expect more efficiency.

Keep exploring ways to accomplish your assignments more efficiently. Some effective time-saving techniques include:

- Keeping form or sample files of material you have prepared or run across in your work or classes, and make sure these files are organized. Ten minutes now can save you hours in the future.

- Reviewing the firm's form or sample files first to see if an appropriate document already exists.

- Asking others if they have handled similar projects.

- Checking with the law librarian for guidance with research projects, both legal and factual.

- Training your secretary to handle the more repetitive parts of projects. Your secretary should also keep projects and files organized for easy retrieval.

ORIENT YOURSELF

If you have ready access to the client files—and can justify spending the time—check through recent correspondence and the rest of the file to determine the current status of the client's matter. Although it may seem unnecessary, in some cases, this step can be critical to completing an assignment accurately. It can alert you to potential problems. It can also save you from asking the lawyer questions that you can answer for yourself, or asking the client for documents and information that have already been supplied.

Reviewing the file also helps when making telephone calls. You will be more knowledgeable about the client and sympathetic to the particular situation. For example, has anyone talked to the client about the matter in the past six months? Is the client in the middle of a corporate acquisition? If so, you may need to allow much more time than usual to obtain the data you need.

The more you see of the big picture, the more you will be able to contribute to the final product.

CHECK FOR NOTES TO THE FILE

Lawyers often write memos to the file and notes documenting telephone conversations which highlight areas of concern or those needing further research. The memos may set forth the status of a project, with an outline of further steps to be taken. Reading these notes and memos can give you valuable information that may not have been conveyed at the assignment meeting.

Most attorneys will generally assume you are (or will become) knowledgeable about the contents of the client's file as part of your job in completing an assignment. Don't overlook the files, both as a resource and a double check on your work.

If you cannot actually read the entire file (or set of files), at least check for notes and any other documents directly affecting the project you've been assigned. If you are not in the habit of looking through the file **first** for these kinds of helping aids, they may just as well not be there.

DO NOT REINVENT THE WHEEL

Most types of documents have been drafted by someone in your law firm before. Since one of your goals is efficiency, ask the assigning lawyer for information regarding sample documents. Keep in mind, however, that in some firms, documents drafted on behalf of one client may be considered the property of that client, and as such, cannot be used for other clients. Be sure to determine your firm's policy on this matter.

If you are drafting a document that might be similar to a document already in the client's file (for example, a board of directors resolution), use that client's existing documents as a starting place before turning to your own standard forms. On the other hand, it may be more efficient to use a document you have already drafted and are familiar with, rather than adapting to the client's format. When in doubt, ask if the attorney has a preference. Either way, do not reinvent the wheel at the client's expense.

KEEP THE CLIENT'S NEEDS IN MIND

Often, the client's satisfaction with your work comes from your knowledge of the client. Consider the following questions about the client's needs:

- Will the client be most comfortable with something that looks familiar?

- Will it be easier for your contact at the client to obtain cooperation and support from others in the organization if you conform your writing style to the client's "corporate dialect"?

- Will the client need to spend time rewriting what you send? Or can they adopt your document as is?

- Does the client want just the minimum required by law?

- Is the client's business only a small shop, or does the client have thousands of potentially litigious employees?

- Are you filling in for reduced staff at the client's office? If so, does this mean the client's budget is tight? Or are you expected to do things just as they would be done in-house?

CHECK YOUR FACTS BEFORE YOU RUN WITH THEM

Before you start a project, it's always a good idea to make a checklist of your tools — all the facts, files and documents necessary for completing the assignment. (Checking the details of the finished assignment itself is dealt with in **Chapter 6**, "Give Your Work One Final Check.") The list of items to check will vary, depending upon your area of expertise. Some examples follow:

- Are the government forms current?

- Are you using the final regulations just issued (not the temporary regulations in the paperback version you keep on your desk)?

- Are the sample documents current?

- Are the supporting documents the final version?

- Do you have all the right dates (i.e., for triggering events, deadlines)?

- Did your secretary follow the instructions on the form?

- Did the client follow the instructions you gave them?

- Were you given what you asked for?

It is easy to overlook these details, especially if you are working on several projects for many different clients. Remind yourself to check them, even if you think the supervising attorney will also be checking. Since you accepted the assignment, it's primarily your responsibility. Lawyers will inevitably remember any past errors in your work when deciding whether to give you new assignments (even if it was someone else who made the mistake).

4

Working with Others

Most supervising lawyers naturally think their assignments are the most important one you have. Unless you tell the attorney otherwise, he or she will probably assume you will be working on that assignment from the minute you accept it until it is completed.

WORKING WITH THE LAWYER

Be Responsive

As soon as possible, return all phone calls. The caller may have information that directly affects what you are doing or when the assignment is due. If you receive a message that your supervising lawyer called, and you have not finished that particular project, don't panic. Resist the temptation to finish the assignment first—return the call **immediately**. The lawyer may be calling to tell you the project is no longer necessary. Or the call may be about something totally unrelated and you will have rearranged your priorities needlessly.

Keep in Touch

Most supervising lawyers naturally think their assignments are the most important ones you have. Unless you tell the attorney otherwise, he or she will probably assume you will be working on that assignment from the minute you accept it until it is completed.

Touch base with the lawyer from time to time as the project progresses (or fails to progress), especially if the project is long and involved. This is particularly necessary if you take every assignment you are offered. You will be juggling many projects, and you want the lawyer to know you have other assignments to work on. A few words about the relative deadlines for each of your projects is sufficient.

Give the lawyer periodic feedback about where you are with the project, what remains to be done, what (if anything) is slowing you down, and when to expect the finished project. If you are working on an assignment which has no immediate deadline—but an emergency arises that will delay your expected progress for a week—say so. If there is only one piece of information you need to complete a project, you may want to let the lawyer decide whether he or she wants the project now, without that piece, or later, with it.

If you find yourself continually putting off a low priority assignment for higher priority work, tell the assigning attorney the situation. Chances are you will not receive new work from that lawyer until the last project assigned to you has been reviewed. On the other hand, perhaps that low priority project has been forgotten entirely.

This latter situation can lead to at least two problems. One possibility is that the attorney may believe the project has already been completed. You don't want the lawyer telling the client it was handled last summer (when she gave it to you), because that's the last thing she remembers. The second possibility is that the client's situation may have changed. The lawyer may not remember to relay relevant changes concerning an assignment given you months ago unless you occasionally remind him that you still have it on the back burner.

A classic example is the case that everyone was sure would never go to trial. If it suddenly heats up, and you haven't prepared the necessary trial notebook, the notebook has now become a project that must be done as soon as possible. If everyone assumes this assignment has already been completed, and you are the only one who knows it hasn't, this can become a serious problem.

Gather Your Questions

Try to gather all your questions about the assignment before interrupting the lawyer. But remember one important **caveat**. You might run across an element of the assignment very early on that can affect which course you take. It may be something which the lawyer did not foresee or merely forgot to tell you. In this case, go back to the lawyer and verify your assumptions before spinning your wheels or heading off in the wrong direction.

Give Your Questions Context

Just because you are immersed in a project does not mean that the attorney who gave you the assignment is as well. He or she will be able to field your questions or comments better if you first describe what ball park you're in. When you ask a lawyer a question or give an update, provide the orientation by first mentioning the client's name and the matter. Then go on to the point you want to make.

For example, don't say, "Do you remember the guy you talked to at Williamson's?" The lawyer will then ask when, and about what, and more than likely, why you want (or need) to know. A better question is: "In that meeting at Williamson's last Friday, do you remember the name of the tax accountant you talked to? I need his report."

When you have questions, spend a minute or two thinking about precisely what it is you need and how to ask your questions clearly and succinctly. Don't make the lawyer have to ask **you** questions to clarify your point. Anticipate likely questions and answer them up front.

A well-phrased question or comment can also elicit more information. Simply stating, "We got the signed papers back from the Jones firm," will get just a quick nod. On the other hand, saying: "We have everything for Friday's filing on Leightner's," may prompt the following response: "I'm going to be out of town Friday so you'd better give everything to me tomorrow."

Constructing your questions and comments to convey background information at the same time can save time and will usually prompt a more informative response.

Respect the Lawyer's Time

Lawyers are under tremendous time pressures, so realize that the attorney may consider your questions as yet another interruption. It is probably one of numerous interruptions she has had to handle that day. Give the lawyer an opportunity to decide whether to take the interruption now or later by letting her know:

- what the questions are about;

- how long they are likely to take;

- what the deadline is; and

- how critical the answers are to finishing the project.

Start the conversation with: "Time for two short questions on the Williamson case?" or "Got about five minutes for some questions about the Waiverly deposition scheduled for tomorrow?"

Generally, you should not bother the lawyer unless you cannot get the answers or information you need anywhere else (short of calling the client). Check with the attorney's secretary first, or look through the file and time records. Ask the lawyer only if it would take much more time to get the information yourself and you know the attorney will have an immediate answer. Then, when you do need to ask a question, the attorney will be more likely to respond quickly because he or she knows that:

■ you have already checked with the lawyer's secretary;

■ you have looked at the time sheets and in the file;

■ you can't get the answer any other way; or

■ you have just run into the lawyer at the water fountain and are trying to save your time without wasting his.

If you have previously shown the ability to ask quick, concise questions, lawyers are more likely to give you the time you need. But, if you are asked to wait until another time, don't leave it up to the lawyer to call you back because she probably won't. Following up is a hassle, which means that you're the one who has to do it.

Keep the Lawyer Informed

While working on a project, a better way to accomplish the purpose of the assignment may occur to you. Or you may notice that something does not make sense. For example, it may appear that the lawyer provided the wrong documents. In such instances, be sure to resolve any questions **before** proceeding. Attorneys expect you to have and use your common sense.

Make sure the lawyer knows all the facts you know and vice versa before assuming "the lawyer knows best." The excuse that "I was just doing what he told me" doesn't fly, especially if it means running up unnecessary time for the client.

For instance, by all means let the lawyer know that preparing a case chronology in the *Acme* matter may take you 10 or 15 hours, but within a week, you can get almost the same information from the document database printouts. Mention that billing 15 hours of your time might appear unreasonable, especially when the client has already paid to have this information available on the computer system. Then let the lawyer decide. He or she may say to hold off on the project. Or, because the printouts will not contain all the necessary information, the attorney may tell you to proceed. Either way, you are better off knowing the whole story.

Let the lawyer know what you are thinking by repeating your assumptions and conclusions. This is especially necessary if the lawyer appears to be disregarding a point you think is important. For example, ask: "You want me to send this letter out **without** Jack's response?" You will be amazed how fast the lawyer corrects this instruction; perhaps he or she did not remember or realize the significance of something you said. Your attention to these details will be appreciated, and after all, it is your job to look for them.

Tailor Your Work to the Lawyer's Preferences

When asked to draft a letter, brief, legal memorandum or other document, determine at the time of the assignment whether the attorney has particular preferences about style or format. She may want to see what you come up with on your own. More likely, however, she wants you to prepare it just exactly as she would.

Do a little research to familiarize yourself with the attorney's style and preferences. You might, for example, read her daily letter or chronological file or form files on your own time, to get a feel for her style. Look for:

■ her level of attention to detail;

■ what tone she uses (high legalese, formal or informal);

■ how she structures the document, beginning and closing paragraphs, transitional phrasing;

■ how she likes documents to look (for example, always double spaced, with lots of room at the beginning and end of pages and between paragraphs, etc.).

People are usually much more comfortable with work that looks like their own.

Copy the Lawyer on Your Letters

Give your supervising attorney the opportunity to know what you did, how you did it, and when. The best way to accomplish this is to send the lawyer "carbon copies" of all letters, memos or other documents you send to a client or are simply related to your assignment. This allows the lawyer to keep up with what is going on and check your performance.

Sending copies of all the documents you author also notifies the lawyer that you have accomplished the assigned task. The "cc:" can act as a reminder about the next steps to be taken, and it can also protect you. It never hurts to have the files show that the attorney knew what you were doing.

Often the lawyer will be reviewing the letter or document before it goes out, making it unnecessary to actually give him or her a copy. A copy in the file will be sufficient. However, the "cc:" message communicates to all recipients that the lawyer knows of the document's contents. Another way to make this abundantly clear is to actually say in the body of the letter or memo that you have discussed this matter with the lawyer or that it has been reviewed by the lawyer.

Obtaining the Lawyer's Signature

When it is necessary to obtain the lawyer's signature on letters or other documents, be sure to forewarn him, or have your secretary remind him as the day approaches (as well as on the day itself), that you need his signature. It is **your** responsibility to get your project completed. It is not up to the lawyer to remember and to be available.

Anticipate the possibility that the lawyer may not be available to sign documents by establishing general rules ahead of time. Should you:

- use the lawyer's signature stamp?

- sign his name and put your initials beside it?

- wait for him to return, however long it takes (and risk missing the deadline, not to mention ruining your evening)?, or

- have the letter or document changed so that it can be signed by someone else who is so authorized?

Lawyers have different opinions on the signature issue, and firms have different policies. Prepare for this problem so you can avoid the headache of hanging around on the due date, not knowing where the lawyer is, and not knowing what he expects you to do in his absence.

Experienced Lawyers Are a Resource

In some firms, most of the "education" that goes on consists of more experienced lawyers pontificating for the benefit of the less experienced ones, or ad hoc brainstorming sessions among peers. This often happens after hours or informally in the hallways of the office. Try to get in on these sessions if you can. Senior attorneys' experiences are valuable resources, and keeping up on the current cases and issues in the office educates you.

If you do not have many opportunities to talk informally with your firm's lawyers about work, use your "free" time to further your projects and awareness of firm issues. For example, when you find yourself in the elevator or by the coffee machine with a lawyer, you might ask for updates or information you need on a project. You can also use this opportunity to fill the lawyer in on the status of your projects.

Know What the Firm Needs

It is important to know what the firm requires regarding the appearance and timeliness of its work product. Your secretary will know more about these things than you do at first and will be a great source of information. Notice how everyone else seems to be getting things done, how documents look, and how long projects take to complete. When in doubt, ask another associate or paralegal.

Know What You Need

The functions that a legal secretary should fulfill are not always immediately obvious to someone starting out in an office. First, you need to learn what a secretary can do. Establish what your expectations for support are and set up general working procedures. Then tell your secretary about your expectations early in your working relationship. Some of these expectations may include:

- Prioritizing projects, especially if your secretary works for more than one person. This means knowing what is important and doing that first, even if that means putting your work ahead of another person's.

- Opening and sorting your mail (opening your mail will provide your secretary with a better idea of what's going on with your work load); date stamping all materials received; making reminder notes for deadlines mentioned in incoming and outgoing letters and memoranda.

- Maintaining and updating a general calendar of important dates and deadlines for meetings, conference calls, due dates for projects, etc.; reminding you of meetings and deadlines; keeping track of your whereabouts, whether in another office of the firm or working out of town.

- Producing your documents; proofreading; double-checking numbers, dates and the spelling of names; using correct grammar and punctuation; using specialized terms correctly; getting the correct names of documents; keeping document formats consistent.

■ Knowing standard operating procedures: returning your marked up documents and giving you a copy to write on so you don't spoil the original; keeping the original document until it is finalized; collating copies before giving them back; making sure any enclosures are included with cover letters (and in the order they are referred to in the letter); filing papers accurately and in a timely manner; keeping sufficient supplies on hand.

■ Knowing office procedures and taking care of items such as getting reimbursements, confirming client/matter numbers, setting up case/matter files; knowing all the ways to send and deliver documents and packages; knowing the hours, costs and rules for using outside delivery, copying and other services.

■ Maintaining records of your clients, their names and addresses and billing numbers; keeping addresses accurate and current; maintaining your daily letter file, time sheets, subject files and client files; coding your client/matter numbers into your telephone; keeping accurate lists of all the parties involved in matters and their current addresses in the front of the client's correspondence file.

■ Taking accurate and complete telephone messages: making sure to give you the correct spelling of the caller's name on phone messages (with notes on pronunciation if needed), and the correct phone number; putting the date (including the year) and the time on the message.

How your secretary handles phone calls deserves particular emphasis. For example, even if the person calling is someone in the firm, your secretary should provide the number on the message slip so you don't have to take the time to look it up. You should also have your secretary screen your telephone calls ("Can I say who's calling?") so you can exercise more control over your interruptions. Also ask your secretary to discreetly find out what the call is about, by saying: "Can I tell her what this is about?" or "Can I tell him what this is in reference to?"

If you are not available, your secretary should take very detailed messages by asking, "Is there something I can help you with?" This will give you the information you need: because the message contains the subject of the original call, you do not have to make a "cold" return call, you will have the file ready and you can avoid another round of phone calls. **Make sure**, however, that your secretary knows not to provide information or send anything out without your okay first.

Delegate All the Appropriate Work You Can

Keep in mind what is appropriate work for your secretary and what is appropriate work for you. Don't try to do the secretary's job. Some secretaries make it so difficult to get your work done, or they do it so badly, that it appears easier to just do it yourself.

Filing is a task that often falls into this category. Do **not** help out with clerical tasks without making very clear that your assistance is temporary. Otherwise, you may find that your secretary thinks this task is part of your job and not his. If you start out assuming that filing is your secretary's job, he will too.

Train Your Secretary

It may seem time consuming to train your secretary, but not providing training will surely cost you more time later. Do not miss any opportunity to tell your secretary what you need and expect, even if you are not accustomed to pointing out other people's mistakes. If you let errors go by without correction, your secretary will naturally assume that what she is doing is right. It will be much harder to change her work later on. If you have a problem with the work, tell her and give instructions for the correct procedure.

Do not forget the other side of the coin, however. Be sure to praise your secretary highly when performance merits it.

Set Up the Routines

If you establish certain ground rules for working with your secretary from the start, both of you will experience a smoother working relationship. Some of the work habit questions to be considered include the following:

- When do you want to be interrupted? Do you want to establish interruption-free times?

- How do you want your secretary to organize your mail (into stacks of client mail, office memos and then junk mail)?

- How much initiative do you expect your secretary to exercise? (For example, for materials that must be reviewed, your secretary can save time by retrieving the files, making copies of documents for you to mark up, and then putting the originals back in the file.)

- Should your secretary wait for instructions on final documents? Or should he proceed to the next step(s)?

Many of your working procedures will depend on your secretary's level of experience. Try to determine quickly how much responsibility your secretary can handle.

Encourage Your Secretary to Ask Questions

Always be receptive to your secretary's questions, no matter how trivial they might seem. It is much better to get things right the first time.

Set guidelines for your secretary to follow for handling your written work. Establish when your secretary should copy verbatim whatever you write or say, when it's okay to go ahead and correct obvious errors, and when it's necessary to stop to ask you questions. The "verbatim" rule, where changes should not be made without telling you, can be a good starting point.

Once you get to know your secretary's work and he or she becomes familiar with your style, these rules can be relaxed. Explain that you would like to start out this way and will adjust the procedure in time. The transition will go more smoothly if you lay out the program in advance.

Make Your Secretary Your Working Partner

A good legal secretary can be a great asset. Let your secretary know that you will respect him for calling your errors to your attention, not the opposite. Help him understand that it is part of his job to protect you from yourself, to know your work and to look at it with a second pair of eyes to ensure that the best possible work goes out. For example, if a number or address is written differently in the same document, your secretary should take the initiative to confirm which one is accurate.

Also let your secretary know that it is his job to correct his own mistakes. You should not have to waste time looking for your secretary's mistakes when you are busy looking for your own. It's hard enough to get the substance right without having to fret over the typos.

Getting the substance right is your job; typing accuracy and the proper appearance of the document are your secretary's responsibilities. You will not have so many drafts to review if your secretary knows he must proofread his own work. Do not let him slip into thinking, "Why should I proofread it when she's going to look at it again anyway?"

Be Flexible

Be flexible about letting your secretary do certain things her way. A good example of this is the organization of the files she will be responsible for maintaining. Another is to ask where on her desk you should put the work you have for processing. Your secretary is more likely to cooperate if she feels comfortable with how things look and when she has a say in how work is accomplished.

Know the difference between your **needs** and your **preferences**, and be flexible with the latter.

Communicate in Advance

Communication saves time and confusion, making everyone's job easier. Nothing annoys a diligent secretary more than having to say "I don't know." She wants to be considered great at her job just as you want to be considered great at yours. The best way you can help with this goal is to keep her aware of what is going on so she can make intelligent choices and be knowledgeable with others.

- Tell your secretary when you will be out of the office or where you will be when you are not at your desk. Also be sure to mention when you expect to return.

- Tell your secretary as soon as possible about important deadlines or upcoming projects. Chances are, she can think of things that can be done ahead of time, like typing up certified mailing receipts and other tasks that might never occur to you.

- Tell your secretary if you will be working on a project with a particular client for a long time. She may want to print up a couple of sheets of address labels in advance, rather than typing single labels each time you send something to the client.

Know Your Secretary's Situation and Cooperate

Be aware of the other pressures on your secretary. For tasks that are routine and boring, give her the information she needs as soon as possible so she can fit these in when she has time. For instance, give her your time records right after the end of the period for which you are recording time (once a day or at least weekly).

The same rule also applies to filing. Give your secretary documents to file little by little as they are finished. Don't wait until the entire project is completed.

If you're not giving your secretary the filing because you do not trust her to put it in the right place, this is your problem, and it is up to you to do something about it. Set a time when you can discuss with your secretary how you want your files organized. Above all, be open and available to her for questions.

Because time sheets and filing are regular and predictable tasks, there is no excuse for you to make them a hassle for your secretary. Letting time sheets or filing pile up in your office only to dump everything on your secretary all at once, expecting her to get it all done in an hour while she's in the middle of other ongoing work, is simply not fair.

Routine projects such as these are much better when done ten minutes here and five minutes there. Your secretary cannot take a whole afternoon or a whole day away from her other work to file documents or enter time records which you should have been giving her all along. Save her patience and goodwill for those desperate times and deadlines which will surely come later.

Involve Your Secretary

Your secretary will have greater job satisfaction if he is actively involved with your client files and work, and you will be free to handle other projects. Find out what he likes to do and find ways of letting him do more of those projects. Telling your secretary every little thing he should be doing can undermine his confidence.

Find ways to give him initiative. For example, if you have some fairly standardized letters, give him a sample letter and the file and ask him to write the first draft. You must, however, learn to supervise and check your secretary's work if you intend to delegate it.

Be Discreet and Professional

Treat your secretary well. Do not convey the attitude that you think you are more important than she is. Secretaries have vast and under-rated power to make or break you at the firm. Your reputation for attention to detail, organization and responsiveness may be attributable solely to your secretary.

Never tell your secretary anything you do not want the world to know. Likewise, never say anything to others about your secretary that you would not want her to hear. Of course, this applies to everyone else working at the firm as well. Rise above office gossip. Be calm and patient.

Personal crises generally subside if you do not "feed" the crisis by talking about them. Take time to give positive feedback and show concern about your secretary's life, but do not feel that it is necessary to win your secretary's friendship. Be sensitive to major problems at home that can affect his work, but do not feel compelled to listen to the daily saga of his love life and family. Set the example: work hard and expect him to do the same.

WORKING WITH PEOPLE OUTSIDE THE OFFICE

Telephone Calls

Whether to call the client. Different lawyers have different preferences about new associates and paralegals contacting clients. Never call a client unless the lawyer has instructed you to do so, or you have specifically informed the lawyer of your need for information and your intention to call. Even when you are fairly comfortable with the client, and the lawyer often expects you to make calls, consider the possibility that the lawyer could have reasons for not wanting you to call in a particular instance.

Consider touching base with the lawyer if you have not talked to the client for some time or if the situation is not a common one. There are several reasons for deferring to the supervising attorney for client contact:

■ The lawyer often has a longer history of dealing with the client; she may be able to get the answers faster.

- Calling to ask for information the firm already has makes the firm look inefficient.

- The lawyer may prefer to call because she has other things to discuss with the client.

- Because the lawyer knows more about the client and the reasons for various actions, she can field the client's questions more easily.

- There may be issues of confidentiality of which you are un-aware. (You do not want to call and leave a message with a secretary that you are calling about the "buy-out of the corpora-tion" when no one in the client's office has been told that the company is being sold.)

- The lawyer may not want you to call because he wants to run things, keep on top of what is going on, or control the messages given to the client about the work.

- The lawyer may not yet know your abilities to communicate over the phone.

- Even if the call is for routine information about which the lawyer would ordinarily not want to be bothered, he may be able to give you pointers on dealing with the client, such as: "He is cooper-ative and has all the information at his fingertips," or "Be prepared to explain everything slowly and clearly because this person is new on the job."

How to talk to a client. If you are not a licensed attorney, do **NOT** give legal advice. If you are a new associate, be sure you **thoroughly understand** your firm's policy with regard to giving legal advice.

When you are speaking with the client, use a tactful, prudent and courteous tone at all times. Do not make personal remarks on initial calls; you can add friendliness later, after you have developed a cordial relationship with the client. Think of your phone as being a party line, and the supervising attorney can pick up and listen to what you are saying at any given moment.

Get to know people at the client's office. Develop a good relationship with the receptionists and secretaries who work for your client and other people you call regularly. Keep a record of their names and call them by name. Encourage your secretary to do likewise. These people can often help you out in a pinch. They understand the trials and tribulations of working in an office and can be good allies when you are under pressure to get things done. They can see that your requests get put at the top of the list and help make sure your questions get answered.

Preparing to call a client. Before you call anyone, make sure you have all your ducks in a row. Just as when asking lawyers for information, make sure you know everything you want to ask and that you cannot get it elsewhere before making your call. Work through the whole project first, collecting all your questions, so you will not have to make repeat calls.

If you must call before you have completed the whole project, alert the client to the fact that this call is about just one aspect of the project that you have to clear up in advance of others, and that you may be calling back later for additional information. Have an idea of where you are going with the project so that you can field the client's inevitable questions.

Giving the best possible service to the client often involves creating the impression that you are doing the client's work and nothing else, or at least that you are on top of her company's problem, attacking it in an organized and efficient manner. Never waste the client's time. There will be enough times when you forget something and have to call back, or when circumstances force you to call at the last minute. Make certain the client can see that these are the exceptions, not the rule, by being prepared whenever you call.

Making telephone calls. When contacting someone for the first time, work out a quick little speech giving your name, your title, the firm name, and the name of the lawyer you are working with in order to orient the client. It is important to pause at this point and ask the person on the other end if he has a minute to talk. People will appreciate your giving them the opportunity to say, "I have someone in my office, can I call you right back?" or "I'm not at my desk, can you hold on?"

If the client will be calling back, remember to take a minute to confirm that he has your telephone number. If you have to give your phone number, repeat your name as well. Even if you introduced yourself at the outset, if the client does not know who you are, he will probably not remember your name. Understand the problem most people have with remembering names and make it easy for them by volunteering yours again.

Next, tell the client what the call concerns, such as "the deposition scheduled for next week." Before you proceed, give the client an opportunity to tell you whether he has the kind of information you are looking for or whether you should be talking with someone else.

Detail what you need and by when, as clearly and succinctly as possible. Try to ascertain ahead of time, or as you proceed, whether your contact understands what you are talking about, or whether you need to orient him to your area of expertise before he can understand you. Let him know how much information you need by the way you phrase your request: "I just want to confirm . . .," or "I want to let you know that I am sending a letter asking you for information . . .," or "Can you give me some facts about the corporation, such as . . . ." Try to anticipate the questions most clients would naturally have during this call, and have the answers—or the sources for finding the answers (such as the file or the instructions)—handy.

If you are calling a government agency, an insurance company or other large organization for information, and you do not have a specific contact, be sure to ask for the name and title of the person (or persons) you speak to. If you are transferred, get the number of the new extension in case you are cut off.

When you leave a message. Prepare ahead of time for the possibility that the person you are calling might not be available. If the information you need is generic enough that someone else might be able to provide it for you, ask to speak to whomever is taking over for your contact (if he or she is out of the office), or to that person's assistant or secretary. Often the assistant or secretary will know best where to find the needed information. If there is no one else working on the project but the information is on file, ask if someone can retrieve it for you.

If you still cannot get the information you need, you will need to leave an appropriate message. It is important to think carefully before revealing the subject of your call to the person answering the phone. When leaving a message, keep in mind the following guidelines:

- **Always** give your telephone number. You do not want to provide any excuses for procrastinating about returning your call.

- Volunteer the spelling of your name and your firm's name.

- If you are returning a call, say so. The secretary or receptionist may get your message through faster—there is no need to guard the boss from an interruption if he or she already wants to talk to you.

- If you are calling a consultant, expert witness, or other persons not associated with the client, also leave the name of your client, so the person you are calling can have that file ready when returning your call.

- If you are calling an insurance company or other corporation which involves identifying the client by number, be sure to leave the appropriate number with your message so that when the person calls back, you can get right to the point without more phone calls.

- Give the message taker some idea of the urgency of your call. Be sure to say that you need a return call today if that is the case, or mention that "sometime this week would be fine."

Finally, since you must plan the rest of your day, and you need to know when you can finish your assignment, be sure to ask, "When do you expect him back?" or "Do you expect her back this afternoon?" The message taker will most likely volunteer a convenient time for you to call back, or offer other relevant information, such as that the person you are calling has just had back surgery and won't be in the office for a month. If you don't ask, you may waste time waiting around for a return call when you could have been getting the needed information from another source.

Answering your phone. Answering your phone at work obviously means more than just saying "hello." You must identify who you are to callers from outside the office. "[Your name] speaking" is short and sweet. Say your name clearly and slowly. That way the person calling does not get halfway into a conversation with you before realizing you are not the person she intended to call.

If your secretary screens your calls, be sure to agree on a procedure for answering the phone. Some firms require a Mr. or Ms. title to be used for their professional staff ("Ms. Johnson's office"). Other firms are less formal ("This is Bob Johnson's office").

Get the basic information. Sometimes you will receive unexpected calls, for example when a lawyer appoints you to field her calls when she is away. As basic as this sounds, be sure to get the caller's name, title and phone number. Keep a note pad handy on your desk for writing down the caller's name when he first says it. If you miss the name, however, don't hesitate to ask for it again. Be sure to confirm the spelling and pronunciation if necessary.

It helps to apologize for asking for that information "again," since it is presumably available in your office, but requesting identifying information is critical and can be a real time-saver:

> "I am sorry, but Ms. McCartney is away from the office. Can I have the spelling of your name and your position with the company again? And your phone number, just in case?"

Handling calls and questions from clients. Sooner or later, the client will get the idea that you are less expensive and possibly more accessible than the senior attorney, so the client may begin calling you with questions. Paralegals and support staff should always keep in mind that they **must NOT give legal advice.** And new associates should be fully aware of firm policy regarding legal advice.

What may seem like an informal and clear-cut question may have further implications of which you are not aware, due either to the law itself or to the client's particular situation. Therefore, scrupulously avoid giving advice or recommendations to, or drawing conclusions for, a client.

Familiarize yourself with your firm's policies for speaking to clients. If you are a new associate, identify yourself as a lawyer new to the firm. If you are a paralegal or a member of the support staff, first remind the client of your position. Always say that you will run the client's question by the attorney.

Check your answer in the law or documents as necessary, and immediately take the question and your suggested answer to the supervising lawyer. Be sure to bring the relevant law sources and files with you, so they will be handy when the inevitable further questions arise. Document your conversation with the lawyer by writing a note to the file. Call the client back as soon as possible so you do not leave him or her wondering.

Don't promise a specific time of day for calling back a client. You never know what will come up between now and then. For example, if a client calls you and you need to talk to the lawyer to answer her question, do not promise to call back in an hour. As soon as you do, you can be assured that the lawyer will be unavailable for the rest of the day.

Avoid the embarrassment of having to call the client back at a promised time without an answer by telling the client: "I will call back as soon as I have an answer." Leave yourself an out and allow for much more time than you really need: "I'll get back to you probably this afternoon, but certainly by the beginning of next week." Then, when you call back in an hour, you look great.

Put a memo in the file which:

- details your conversation with the client;

- references your conference with the lawyer;

- summarizes the conclusions reached; and

- includes any information from the client on which those conclusions were based.

Always prepare this memo as soon as possible or it might not get done. Dictating the memo is easiest, or you can scribble a quick memo for your secretary to decipher. Another alternative is to send a computer mail message containing the above facts to the lawyer, which you can print out for placement in the file.

Make sure the date on the final memo is the day you wrote it, **not** the day it was typed. This is contrary to most documents, where the date the document is typed and goes out is the important date. Because memos to the file are not going anywhere but the file, they tend to be typed much later.

Be sure that your secretary knows—and understands the importance of—the date the memo was originally generated. You can ensure this by mentioning the actual date of the conversation in the text of the memo: "I received a call from the president of Atlas Company today (Wednesday, April 23, 1993), requesting information about...." Vague references to dates such as "yesterday" or "last week" will not accomplish your goal.

> **Specific Advice for Paralegals**: After clients go through this routine a couple of times, they will learn they should not call you with legal questions. Sometimes, however, you can serve a valuable role by helping a client determine whether the question at hand is a legal one. For example, the question may be one which is answered in the instructions to the form he is working on, with which you will naturally be more familiar. Client questions can involve difficult situations; your area of legal expertise and your discretion will play large roles in handling them properly.

Confidentiality and telephone calls. Every person working in a law firm knows that work for clients is confidential. Very rarely is that confidentiality breached purposely; it usually happens by accident. Telephone calls can present many opportunities for such accidents to occur.

Do **not** assume, in an overzealous attempt to be helpful, that the person calling you is actually authorized to receive the information requested. If someone calls you out of the blue, ask where he or she got your name.

Once, a financial officer for a company that recently purchased a division of our client's company called to ask for a copy of the annual reports for our client's pension plans. He said that the IRS had contacted him for copies. I happened to have just what he was looking for right on my desk. Because I always see commercials for his company on national TV, I was impressed. But I said I would check and get back to him. After I talked to the lawyer and the client, it turned out that our client did **not** want to reveal the financial status of its pension plans to the buyer. I called back and asked the financial officer to send the IRS's request to us for handling.

Always check with the lawyer and/or the client **before** revealing information to **anyone**.

Writing Letters

Purpose of cover letters. Cover letters are the signposts of the paper trail. They verify that legal information and documents were provided, and also establish when. The goal of cover letters is to let the correspondence file show exactly what is going on, in a way that can be understood by those unfamiliar with the project both now and in the future. Do this by providing the context, even though it may seem obvious and redundant to you now. The context is not obvious to others, nor will it even be clear to you in a year or so, unless you make it clear now.

When writing a cover letter, don't just say, "enclosed are the papers we discussed." Down the road, that cover letter will lose its value because it does not clearly detail what was sent. Cover letters often get separated from their enclosures. The enclosed documents themselves may be marked up, highlighted, executed, filed or forwarded, but the cover letter just gets stuck in the correspondence file. Therefore, identify—in great detail—what you are sending:

- include the full and accurate title of the document;

- specify the date of the document being sent;

- mention the status of the document, for example, whether it is a draft or in final form; and

- tell why you are sending it.

It is particularly helpful to say "as you requested," if applicable, to let the client's secretary know this is something the client wants. This is also a subtle reminder that fees in connection with providing this information were incurred at the client's request.

Who writes the cover letter. Sometimes the lawyer will want to draft the cover letter because, for example, she knows what she wants and can dictate it faster than the time it would take to go through the review and correction process with you. Or, other matters may need to be discussed with the client and the enclosures will be only part of that letter.

Often, however, you can save the lawyer time, either by drafting a letter in his style for his signature, or by sending it under your own signature without bothering the attorney. Confirm ahead of time which procedure the lawyer prefers.

Purposes of other letters. Letters serve many purposes in addition to transmitting documents. They can request or provide information and ask or answer questions. Common purposes for other letters include the following:

■ The supervising lawyer may be delegating and delineating responsibility, making sure everyone knows who is doing what. Detailing plans in a letter can prevent someone from discovering (when it is too late), that "my notes indicate that you were responsible for filing that form."

■ The lawyer may be recording and documenting events and decisions to show that your firm and your client were duly diligent. This creates a paper trail showing that you took care of problems as soon as you became aware of them. (Remember that some work by law firms involves being aware of and periodically aiding the client's defense against possible lawsuits.)

■ The lawyer may be orienting a client to a process over a period of time. Referring to past or upcoming steps in that process helps the client remember and be prepared for the next steps.

If you write a letter requesting action, state precisely what is required and who should take action. An aid in getting the reader to do what you want quickly is to orient him or her to the subject matter and explain why your request is necessary. You may be working in a specialized area of the law, but the people with whom you correspond may deal with many different subjects. Do not assume that the reader will know what you are talking about; write a sentence or two to lead into the subject.

Specific Advice for Associates: If you are writing a letter giving advice, providing a status report or a legal opinion, or any other letter which represents the firm, be sure you review firm policy and prior letters from the firm for style, content, form and procedure before you start drafting.

Drafting letters for the lawyer's signature. When you are drafting a letter for a lawyer, you should first become familiar with:

- the lawyer's writing style;

- the tone the lawyer uses to explain something to a client;

- what kind of introductory and closing paragraphs the lawyer prefers;

- how the lawyer handles transitions between topics; and

- how the lawyer structures a letter to deal with several related or unrelated issues.

Read through the client's correspondence file when time and the client's pocketbook allow. One example of how the lawyer's style may differ from yours is in the tone. The attorney might be more authoritative and use the word "I." You, on the other hand, might be more formally polite and use "we," if only because you have not yet met the client.

Keep your audience in mind. When you write a letter, gear it to the person who will be receiving it. When you assume the reader is familiar with the procedures you are discussing, say that and tell the recipient to ask you if there are questions. If you know the recipient's attitude is that he or she cannot be bothered, consider highlighting a few relevant phrases so you stand a better chance of getting a response.

If the reader is in a support capacity and totally unfamiliar with the subject area, consider using a yellow post-it note to flag the most critical area of the letter. The note should give specific guidance, such as "Be sure to file with Department of Labor." Then draw an arrow pointing to the paragraph which discusses this requirement and gives the address. This is particularly helpful when your letter covers a topic that you have not previously discussed with the recipient.

It is best, however, to use letters only to "paper the trail," and not as the sole method of communication. Avoid possible mistakes that you can foresee.

Precautions for writing letters. Remember the following precautions when beginning to draft letters. Checking this list is especially important when you're drafting letters requesting action.

- remind the client of deadlines;

- tell the client to review the document;

- point out dates, names or other things that have changed or that might require particular attention;

- warn the client of points you have seen other people overlook;

- alert the client to legal requirements of which he or she might not be aware;

- spell out your assumptions;

- tell the client any caveats or exceptions; and

- always invite questions and comments.

Particularly when the purpose of your letter is to tell the client what action is required, make it clear that your advice is offered merely to be helpful, and that it does **not** absolve the client of its own responsibilities.

There have been several situations in the practice of employee benefits when clients routinely forget some of the wrap-up documentation. For example, they forget to execute the proposed qualification amendment within 90 days after they have the IRS's favorable determination letter, or they forget to keep filing annual returns on the trust after the plan is terminated (which is required for as long as there are assets in the plan).

Clients need to be reminded of these types of specific steps, but in doing so, be sure you do not give the impression that this is all they have to do. In that connection, using the phrase "among other things" is helpful. You do not want it to appear that you have taken on the task of doing or reminding the client of everything.

Other precautions to keep in mind when drafting letters follow:

- **Never** say anything in writing about which you are not absolutely certain. Always allow for the possibility that your recollection or your understanding may be wrong. Use "presumably" or "apparently" or "I understand" if you cannot verify the statement directly, or if the information is something the lawyer told you.

- Use caution before referring to an issue as a "problem." If someone to whom the letter is not addressed reads it, you do not want this person to think there might be a "problem" with the buyout or the pension plan's coverage, for example. Cast the letter in innocuous terms that will serve your purpose without raising red flags.

- When sending documents (or other items) at the client's request, say so in your letter. You want to make clear who initiated the request for which the client will be charged.

Importance of discretion. Never put anything in writing that would embarrass a client or anyone else, even if the purpose of your letter is to correct an error.

Once, a client filed annual reporting forms for a number of years, incorrectly stating in each form that the plan year was "August 1 to September 30," a 14-month period. The temptation to correct the client was almost overwhelming, but instead, our letter said: "as we discussed, I will be using an October 1 to September 30 plan year." This language satisfied the only valid purpose for mentioning the dates in the letter, which was to confirm which 12-month period would be used. Anyone wondering about a mistake like this can look at the file and will appreciate, as did this client, your discretion.

Lawyer review of letters. When the lawyer has you sign a letter, assume he or she wants to see it before it is sent. This is true unless it really is just a cover letter, and/or sending it without the lawyer's review has been specifically okayed. Final review of the letter lets the lawyer:

■ know the letter's done;

■ have a second chance to clarify, correct or add to what was previously communicated to you;

■ control the quality of the work product;

■ gain further knowledge about the work in case the client calls; and

■ review and gain confidence in your work.

Shortcuts. It is not always in the client's or your own best interest to take the time to prepare a formal letter. If you don't have time to dictate or draft a cover letter, you can send the document with a note along with your business card. Keep a record of what you sent and when you sent it by having your secretary copy the first page of the transmitted document, showing the **dated** note and your card.

Better yet, train your secretary to draft, sign and send simple or commonly occurring cover letters, such as:

"Enclosed [as you requested] [for your information, review and/or files] are copies of the depositions of Smith and Jones in the *Acme* case, which were taken on June 28th and December 6th, respectively. If we can be of further assistance, please call."

Teach your secretary the technique of specifically identifying—by name and date—what is being sent and why, and to use your preferred closing sentence.

Mechanics. Always use the subject matter "Re:" line to orient the recipient and anyone receiving a copy of the letter, as well as the person filing the letter. Include standard identifying information in the "Re:" line. In letters to the Internal Revenue Service on a pension plan, for example, include the employer identification number, plan number and IRS File Folder Number. For a letter to an insurance company, include the contract name and number.

A shorthand description of the subject will probably mean more to most people, however: "1992 Annual Minutes for the XYZ Corporation," or "*Smith* Dissolution Order to Show Cause." For consistency (and to avoid confusing the client), check the "Re:" line the lawyer uses on related correspondence and use the same one.

Train your secretary to always put your initials on letters you draft, since that is usually the only credit you will get. The lawyer's initials should be in caps, next are your initials in caps, and then the secretary's in lower case: "JFL:NP:jlr." Also, make sure your secretary makes copies of the letter for both the lawyer's and your own daily letter (or chronological) files.

You will also need to "carbon copy" the same people at the client's office (and their consultants, etc.) whom the lawyer usually copies on letters to the client. Do not leave it up to the lawyer to remember and then have to add it. It is better to let the attorney delete it if it does not apply.

Advance Warning and Follow Up

Let the client know it's coming. Always consider calling the client before sending a letter requesting information. This way, you are more likely to get a prompt response because the client is prepared: he knows the letter is coming, who the letter is from, what it's about, and how long he has to fulfill the request. Then you can start your letter "as we discussed," which is easier than working through a detailed introductory paragraph.

If you do not give advance notice, the client may put your letter at the bottom of the pile until he has time to figure out what you are talking about by reading your letter (no one ever reads letters until they have to). If you've prepared the client in advance, he does not have to read the letter but can quickly forward it to the person who is really going to do the work. This way, you make the client look and feel efficient because he gets that piece of paper off his desk, and you'll receive your answers faster.

Another advantage of calling the client in advance: if the client is on the lookout for something you are sending but does not receive it, he can let you know. Of course, you cannot rely on the client remembering that you were planning to send a letter. Therefore, your follow-up system must be in place.

Follow up on requests for information. If you are in charge of getting information from other people, calendar a reminder to follow up with them after a reasonable period. You will often find that they have forgotten, lost, or never even received your request. Or, they may be perfectly aware of your request but, for whatever reason, they will not get around to answering it unless you make them miserable first. For some people, the rule is "remind them early and often."

Signatures and Documents from Clients

Obtaining signatures from the client. It is a good idea to check early on whether the right people at the client's office will be around to sign documents. This is especially important in the summer and around the holidays. There is nothing worse than having a project all done except for the signature, and then being told the client is on vacation for a month.

When sending documents to clients for signature, do not just say "sign." Tell them to "**review** and sign." Also, tell the client who should sign, and what title should be used. This way, if the person signing happens to have more than one corporate function or title, the right one is used. Also tell the person signing to fill in the current date. As soon as you receive the signed documents back, double-check them to make sure they are properly signed and completed, so you can promptly correct any errors.

Save the client's markups. Of course you will keep the client's correspondence and signed documents in the file, but you should also save less formal papers. If the client "markups" (revised documents) are relatively short, attach them to the appropriate transmittal letter in the main correspondence file. If the markups did not come with a letter, write on the documents who they are from (i.e., who was responsible for preparing them), and the date they were received. Then put them in the "working papers" or another specially designated file, such as "Census data for pension plan from Ted Higgins at Specialty Services, September 1986."

This rule also applies to document changes transmitted during telephone conversations. Keep a record of what information you obtained, from whom and when. A note in the correspondence file or working papers file is fine for this purpose.

Good record keeping can be especially important if you are identifying "typos" or computing errors, and fixing them as you go. It may turn out that the error was not where (or what) you thought it was. You might need to refer back to the original numbers, even long after the original document has been completed. You must, therefore, always save the backup data prepared and supplied by others so you will be able to reconstruct what happened.

Read the correspondence you receive. When you receive correspondence, **read it carefully**. Do not assume that it says what it is supposed to say, or what you thought it was going to say. This may seem like unnecessary advice, and I wish it were, but since this mistake is made often (and I make it too often myself), it bears repeating. Just as you assume your letters will be read, you must carefully read all the correspondence you receive.

You know how frustrating it is when you get something back that is incorrect and say to yourself or the lawyer, "But I **told** them in the letter . . . ." It may just be a transmittal letter and after all, transmittal letters say basically the same thing ("Enclosed please find . . ."). You must, however, allow for the possibility that the client did not adequately convey over the telephone what was being sent. It may also be that the client thought of something else after speaking with you and simply tucked it into that letter with a sentence like, "I assume this will be acceptable unless I hear otherwise from you."

Document the results. It is important to document the results of your work. Those using the file after you may not be familiar with the circumstances and will need to know the outcome of any problems or questions. Contemporaneous documentation of results also has the most reliability.

Take the time to document the resolution of any questions that were raised in the client's correspondence. A handwritten note on the letter itself or a memo detailing the telephone conversation is sufficient. You do not want the last thing in the file to be the client's question to you with no indication of how, or if, you handled it.

5

While Working on the Assignment

Develop methods to keep track of the assignments you are given and the status for each of them. Often, when a lawyer gives you a task, she forgets about it because the ball is no longer in her court.

ORGANIZING YOURSELF

Work Planning

Just as you should never leave at the end of the day without completing your time sheets, you should not start any day without specific work goals in mind. Placing a list in the middle of your desk before going home the night before is a good idea. It does not matter when or how you do the planning (visualizing your day ahead of time while in the shower or commuting works well), as long as it enables you to hit the ground running when you reach the office. If you've planned your work day, you can usually get some good work done before the interruptions start. As a result, you'll feel good about making progress, and can carry that feeling through the inevitable roadblocks.

In contrast, a few unproductive hours at the beginning of your work day can make the rest of the day unbearably long and arduous. If you haven't prepared a battle plan into which you can just barely fit all the things you have to do, you will be at the mercy of people who stop by to chat, trips to the vending machines, and the first piece of paper that crosses your desk or mail message that pops up on your computer terminal.

Look at the most productive lawyers you know. Chances are they put pressure on everyone around them by setting (sometimes) arbitrary deadlines which keep everything moving double-time. You can be certain they have a goal in mind for each minute of the day.

Prioritize Your Assignments

Develop methods to keep track of the assignments you are given and the status for each of them. Often, when a lawyer gives you a task, she forgets about it because the ball is no longer in her court. It is critical that you carry through. Just because the supervising lawyer is ultimately responsible does not mean it is up to her to check the status of every project with you or remind you to do the work.

You can pick from a variety of systems that will help you keep track of your projects:

- the "pile system"—you have everything necessary for a single project in a stack that you keep shifting around your desk or office;

- the "list system"—on a note pad, you rewrite your goals every day or two;

■ the "post-it system" — you line up post-it notes along your bookshelf, rearranging them from time to time to reflect changing priorities or progress;

■ the "card file system" — you note each project on a card, and you shuffle through the cards frequently;

■ the "computerized reminder system" — using either a calendar software package or date reminder pop-ups to keep projects on track, you reschedule due dates as events and priorities change.

Whatever system you use, you must pay regular attention to it. Never put away a project in the file or in a drawer without preparing a separate reminder or note about it, because otherwise, you will never rediscover it in time. Never assume you will remember to look for it "as soon as I finish this big project," or the next time you organize, or at any other time. It will not resurface unless you make specific provisions to check on it.

Frequently reevaluate the order in which you intend to handle your assignments. Guard against putting off undesirable or lengthy assignments. If you hate to make phone calls, make them anyway, the minute you think of them. Mulling over them only makes them worse. Getting the "ugliest" thing off your desk first thing in the morning is sage advice.

Set the Stage

You don't want to finally clear your desk for a big project only to find you have to wait for the file to come back from storage before you can begin. Take a spare moment during the day to prepare the stage for the next assignment before the one you are currently working on is completed. This way, you are conscious of what you will be doing next and can eliminate that lull after a major project is completed when you ask yourself, "Now what?"

Before you are ready to start on a new project, have your secretary:

■ gather all relevant files and documents;

■ prepare new working file folders;

■ make lists of key players (and their telephone numbers) if appropriate;

■ confirm the correct client/matter billing number;

■ scan (or type) into the word processing system the samples or documents you will need;

■ retrieve any appropriate sample documents from computer archives.

Keep the Pressure On

If you have only a few assignments on deck, try to avoid the tendency to slow down and stretch them out to fill the time available. Continue to work as hard as you can to get the projects done. Inevitably, next time you walk down the hall, three people will stop you with new projects and you will have to push those last few assignments to the end of the line again. Chances are they were not priorities, otherwise they would not have been the last things on your list to do. A project can turn into tar sitting on the back burner and you may never be rid of it.

If you find yourself bogging down, switch to an assignment that you can finish quickly and feel good about. Or solicit feedback from a lawyer on your progress and ask for a few new assignments to juggle. It is remarkable how much more quickly you can work if you have a little too much to do.

Use Lists and Reminders

Lists. Have your secretary keep a running list, in a centralized place (such as the inside front cover of the correspondence file), of the names, titles, addresses, and telephone numbers of all the parties involved. Make sure your secretary knows to keep these lists current, especially as new parties become involved and addresses change.

You might also want to have your secretary maintain a list of all vendors and service providers you or your firm ordinarily uses. These can include court reporters, corporate formation services, special office supply companies, etc. Having these names and phone numbers handy can be a blessing when you're pressed for time.

Checklists. On long and complicated projects, draw up a timetable of tasks and check off your progress on data gathering and document production. (The computer is a great tool for creating and modifying checklists.) Referring back to old checklists will help you coordinate new, similar projects.

On your checklists, note what further information you need as thoughts occur to you. Share this checklist with the lawyer; she might want you to keep a checklist for her also. This will help coordinate your efforts, and provide a centralized place to return when you get interrupted with more pressing assignments.

One word of caution: do **not** let keeping a checklist bog you down. Make it simple, don't write a diary of events. Restricting checklists to one page will force you to be concise.

Reminders. Take time to set up reminders on the computer as ideas for follow up occur to you and as due dates are set. Include the detailed information you need while you have it handy:

- the person's name and telephone number;

- the subject of the reminder;

- any forms or other documents may be required; and

- the dates or deadlines involved.

This way, you won't have to drag the file out again when it comes time to follow up. Accomplishing the object of the reminder can be reduced to a short phone call instead of becoming a major project.

Handling Interruptions

New associates and paralegals rarely have control over who stops in, who calls, and who expects immediate action on his or her work. You generally have little leeway to say "I won't be taking any calls this morning." You may not even have an office door to close. When you do get interrupted, note where you are so you can start right in again where you left off. Don't add to the confusion by interrupting yourself to answer electronic mail messages, make phone calls, read your junk mail, or by letting your secretary interrupt you for things that can wait. The most important thing is to keep track of all those frequently short, but client-billable interruptions. If you don't, you will certainly lose a lot of billable time each day.

If someone stops by to chat, go ahead and chat for a minute (otherwise you will go crazy), but don't put your pencil down, straighten up, stretch and lean back in your chair. These are signals that you are ready for a break. Stay poised over your work or half turned away to get something you need from a file or drawer.

When you need to end a conversation, stand up and walk the person to the doorway of your office. If you are ready for a break, walk with the person to the water fountain, which is an easy way to control the length of the break. If interruptions happen too often, delay looking up when someone comes in to your office. Consider keeping a pile of stuff on the visitor's chair in your office. Arrange for your secretary to call you on the telephone if a notorious talker has been in your office more than a few minutes, so you can sidetrack the conversation and get back to work.

Avoid developing habits that can interfere with your productivity. As addictive and enjoyable as these little things are—and as necessary as they may be in moderation—it still takes time to go to the snack bar or beverage machine, take a cigarette break, or follow up on your co-workers' life traumas. If you're bored, it is easy to allow yourself to do these things. When you need a break, try instead to get human contact by following up with a client or lawyer, or talking to a lawyer about more work to keep yourself on track.

Record All Your Time

The importance of recording your time and submitting it for billing **cannot** be overstated. It is critical that you record your time **daily**, **accurately**, and **in detail**. This is the only way the firm can be paid for the services you perform. Failing to accurately and fully record your time can be viewed as akin to stealing, either from the firm or from clients, depending on which side you err. It is grounds for dismissal in some firms. You are also ultimately hurting yourself, since the firm is understandably highly concerned with billable hours.

Keeping time records is not a chore of secondary importance that can be put off indefinitely. Nor are time records the proper forum for candid disclosure of problems and errors, either yours or anyone else's. Time records must be handled with the same diplomacy, skill and attention to detail that applies to all your work.

There is a certain public relations aspect to time records. Your time descriptions are what supervisors and lawyers look at to learn what you are doing, and what clients look at to find out whether your work is worth paying for. It is the summation of all your efforts. **Sell yourself and your work**. Make everyone reading your time descriptions think they cannot live without you. Your objective is to make the reader say, "She did all that in only 2.00 hours?" and **not** "Is that all she did in 2.00 hours?"

Write down all the details as you work, because there is no foolproof way to reconstruct events after the fact. This is especially true if you have many projects to work on in a day and many interruptions. The following guidelines should be considered, together with the specific guidelines and policies established by your firm or department:

- Keep the book, diary or tablet on which you record time right by your elbow along with your pencil, **not** put away somewhere in a drawer where you will forget to use it.

- Do **not** start any new project without making an entry in your time records.

- Do **not** attend to an interruption without looking at your watch and taking a second to note it.

■ Do **not** let two hours go by without making an entry.

■ Do **not** leave the office without fully accounting for that day's time. And that means **every** minute.

One great way to discipline yourself and improve your productivity is to keep in mind that time records allow you—and everyone else—to know where your time goes.

When writing entries, use verbs with both active and positive connotations:

review, survey, examine, assess

research, investigate, analyze, explore

develop, amplify, augment

draft, delineate, brief

edit, revise, annotate

complete, finalize, conclude, perform

design, specify, originate

create, produce, devise

formulate, define, stipulate

organize, plan, outline, itemize

Refer to concrete actions and specific events, especially those in which the client participated:

telephone calls

meetings

conferences

discussions

Never list clerical work unless it is clearly required after regular office hours or in order to meet a deadline. Even then, since it will not ultimately be apparent to the billing attorney or client that the time spent was after hours (it just becomes part of the total), try to spice up your time descriptions with tasks that sound substantive, not clerical:

- Don't say "copy, collate, and staple." Instead, say "review and finalize."

- Don't say "proofread, check enclosures, and take to mail room." Instead, say "supervise production of final opinion letter."

- Don't say "look for." Instead, say "research," "locate" or "retrieve."

You should never repeatedly record time for "filing" or "sorting" or "making a list" or "sending reminder notices" or doing anything else your secretary can do. While you are writing time descriptions on your time sheets, ask yourself: Is this something for which the client would want to pay $75 to $125 an hour? Or is this a task that my secretary could be handling?

Overtime

A former co-worker had an attitude toward working late that I have come to appreciate. She did not ever **plan** to work overtime, although of course she did so when necessary. She just planned to work "seven and a half good ones" every work day. By thinking, "I'll make up for this by staying late or by coming in next Saturday," you can end up procrastinating about the work at hand.

Yes, there is the danger that you won't make up that time, but it is more dangerous to allow yourself the attitude that it is okay to not do it now. If you instead tell yourself to work "seven and a half good ones," you will get the most out of the time you spend at work, you are less likely to have to give up your free time, and you get extra billable hours when you actually do have to stay late. You do not wind up spending seemingly endless hours at work with nothing much to show for it.

To the extent you can control the situation, it is better to work steadily than to put yourself under pressure by playing catch up. Those of us who have worked through deadline crunches know that, in the long run, working around the clock averages out with the temporary paralysis that comes after burn out.

Keep Your Office Neat

This may sound obvious, but so many people have messy offices that mentioning it seems necessary. There are many good reasons for keeping your office neat as you go along, as opposed to shoveling it out once a month.

If you take a few minutes to label the client's papers and your notes and drafts for filing immediately after every project, you can usually charge that time to the client for whom you did the project (if this is in accordance with firm policy), just as you can charge for the time it takes to write time sheets if you record your time as you are working. If you leave the cleanup and time recording on all your projects for some time later, like the end of the week, these tasks take considerably more time which cannot then be easily differentiated or allocated to clients.

Neatness also promotes confidence in your organizational abilities and makes you look efficient. People will feel more comfortable about giving you papers if they think there is some likelihood of seeing them again. Lawyers, more than most people, see order as a prerequisite to giving you their work. The impression you give is, to some extent, as important as your actual work product. In addition, if you have orderly work habits, you are probably less likely to make, or at least more likely to catch, your own mistakes.

Then there is always the unexpected. I once had what I thought would be a routine appointment with the eye doctor, who had me admitted to the hospital then and there for a detached retina, saying I could not return to work for six weeks. I'll leave the resulting chaos to your imagination.

Keep Up with the Little Stuff

If you get behind on things like reading advance sheets or setting up and maintaining your samples files, forget it. Don't expect that you will have time to go back and fix the past before correcting the present. Just settle for keeping up from now on. If you are not organized enough to keep up with the little things on a regular basis, chances are you will never want to sacrifice the weekends of work it will take to reconstruct what you should have been doing all along.

Try to set up systems and schedules you can live with. For instance, you could set up a schedule to read advance sheets Tuesdays and Thursdays at lunch or while you are waiting for group meetings to start. Or carry them with you everywhere so when you are stuck waiting for a bus, an elevator or a doctor, you will have them readily at hand.

Have your secretary set up your personal files. Later, she can give you a list of the file headings so you can quickly note the file name on the document as you review it. This allows you to quickly determine where every new document or sample should go. Do not wait until you have time to do the superior job you know you could do yourself because, your best intentions notwithstanding, it is not likely to happen.

Major Project Wrap Up

Clean up and organize your office the same evening a big project is finished. Not only will you be in a better mood when you return, but you might run across a mistake you made on that project while you still have time to correct it.

Keeping track of your time is even more important than usual during high-pressure projects. When you are swamped, it is easy to forget to record your time. It's also easy to justify postponing that task (after all, you have "real" work to do). But the more projects you are handling, the harder it is to reconstruct everything you did after the fact. It is horrible to finally make it through to the end of a major project and find you do not have the records to show for all your time well spent.

Maintain a list of things you are telling people you will do "as soon as this deadline is past," otherwise you will never remember them all. You'll want to be able to start right in again after you recover from the big project. You also want people to know that when you say you will get back to them, you will.

TIPS FOR WORKING ON THE ASSIGNMENT

Keep Track of Your Assumptions and Decisions

When an assignment requires you to decide how to achieve a certain result, identify your assumptions, determine what you must do, and what steps you do not need to take. Detail as well the decision-making process used to achieve this result.

Regardless of whether your assumptions and decisions actually appear in the final product, the lawyer will need to know that you have indeed considered all the relevant possibilities, and to check that your assumptions are correct. This approach also helps you develop your reasoning process, and keeps you from going around in circles.

Find out how the lawyer wants you to communicate your assumptions and when. For example, your assumptions might be conveyed to the lawyer in:

- a discussion after reviewing the project and the relevant papers, but before you begin drafting;

- notes accompanying the completed project;

- a discussion at the time you return the completed project; or

- a memo, formal or informal, that accompanies the completed project.

Get the Details Right

It may seem that you have to be responsible for everything: deciding how to accomplish the task, doing the research, preparing first and final drafts, obtaining all the information and filling out all the forms, editing the final product, cleaning up all the details, and finally, making sure the document is accurate and mailed on time to the appropriate person or filed with the court. It's true, you **are** responsible for everything. The supervising lawyer will conduct a review or two of your work and will often sign the final documents, but the rest is yours. Don't let yourself forget that you are responsible for the accuracy of the smallest details as well as the appearance of the finished product.

A good way to stay on top of the details is to have all the files handy when you are working on the project. As you are gathering the information, double-check it then and there. When you write down a piece of information, look back at the original, check an alternate source, and carefully compare your information to these sources before moving on to the next question. Then when you are done, you **are** done. Do not write down what you think the information is and expect yourself to remember where it was, that it was a guess, and that you have to go back and check it later.

It is often more efficient to take the time to run through the assignment thoroughly once, verifying what you can and flagging the few open issues as you go, than it is to go through it once quickly and then again later (and more slowly) because you have left the verification of details for last. This second pass through the assignment also happens to be one of those boring tasks that often gets put off, bogs you down, and if you don't watch it, might not get done at all. In short, guard against doing the interesting part first and leaving the cleanup for later.

Get into the habit of double-checking your work, the work of others (such as copies produced by the copy center), and materials returned from outside the office. If you do this, you can be secure in your work and others will also have confidence in your work. Do **not** take shortcuts, or make unsupported assumptions. If you do not check and double-check for accuracy, you will not be able to rely on the work you have done in the past.

Check Phone Numbers

Do not give someone a telephone number you have never used. It is embarrassing to have left out the extension or mistake the extension for a direct dial number. It's even worse to give someone a disconnected number. This is an excellent illustration of the attention to detail that is absolutely necessary.

Finish the Project

When your work is often edited by lawyers, you may begin to feel that your end product is always just a draft. You could be lulled into leaving some of the wrap up for later, assuming you will have another shot at the assignment after the lawyer gives you his initial comments. Surely as soon as you do this, a lawyer will rely completely on your work or send it out as is.

When mistakes surface, as they tend to do, you will be asking yourself why in the world you did not check this or complete that. Keep in mind that the wrap-up step—checking those dull details like effective dates and cross references—is what the lawyer expects and relies on you to do.

Say you fail to follow through with the details on a particular project and there are obvious discrepancies which the lawyer finds only when trying to finish off the work at the eleventh hour. This is the second-to-worst scenario. The worst scenario is if the discrepancies are **not** obvious and the work goes out **without** correction.

Because you started relying on the attorney to finish your work, you've missed an opportunity to be of real assistance by highlighting for the lawyer's benefit any apparent problems (accompanied by a list of possible solutions), long before the deadline. Instead, you have just given the lawyer the impression that your work cannot be trusted, so it would be wise not to seek further help from you. Even worse, by sending out incorrect documents or information, you may have caused the firm to lose the argument, the case or the client.

In addition to the importance of the ultimate accuracy of the project and convenience to the lawyer, there is a more subtle reason for wrapping up the little stuff. Failure to follow through and complete the wrap up short-circuits an important part of the work process. Sometimes, the facts discovered while going through the files and documents to finish an assignment can change your approach to an assignment. They may remind you of other relevant issues and enable you to resolve them, or at least note them for discussion with the lawyer. If you discover that you do not have a document or file that is needed to wrap up the project, get it. It is astonishing how often running across something in the file triggers further thoughts and actions. Do not undermine the process by putting off wrapping up the details until it's too late.

Legal work is not an exact science. Develop all the good habits you can to create the environment in which "luck" can happen, for it is not really luck at all, but the result of conscientious attention to detail.

Use Dictation Equipment

Unless you have serious editing to do, it is always easier to prepare documents using dictating equipment. All routine letters should be dictated. Dictation is also good for quickly memorializing telephone calls for the file. Learning how to do it now will save you countless hours.

Before you begin dictating, first make sure you have everything in front of you: the files, the correspondence, and your notes. Start out your dictation by telling your secretary what it is you are dictating. Specify whether this will be a draft or a document that will probably go out as is.

Don't worry about dictating everything perfectly, but do correct obvious errors as you go along. At the end of each document, mention:

- to whom the carbon copies will go;

- whether you want your secretary to make all the copies now, as for a final letter, or just one copy to mark up;

- list the enclosures if it is not clear from the context of the letter what they are and where to find them; and

- you may even mention where to file the final document.

Tell your secretary when you have reached the end of each document, and when you've gotten to the end of the tape. If you don't use the whole tape, do **not** rewind it. That way your secretary can determine how far the dictation goes on the tape, as well as how much time to allocate for transcribing it.

In time, you'll find that dictating your documents becomes easier. Don't get discouraged. Often the letter you think will have to be changed radically comes out just the way you want it.

If you have a computer at your desk, you may find (as many attorneys and legal assistants have) that drafting documents directly on the computer is the most efficient method for creating documents. Personal preference and the resources available to you will determine whether you draft on the computer, hand write documents or dictate and give the draft to your secretary to type. You should, however, be open to learning new techniques as computer technology becomes more available. Don't let your current habits limit you simply because new ones are uncomfortable at first.

Keep Track of Where You Find Things

Whether you are reviewing documents, a file, an article, or cases, jot down the cite in your notes while you have it available. It saves time later when you are discussing or writing about it, to have the reference readily at hand. You can double-check sources more easily, and quickly find the actual language to give the supervising attorney if necessary.

Make Notes to the File

It is very helpful to write yourself notes that will clue you in to special situations later. Notes only work, however, if you can actually find them when you need them and if you can figure them out. It can be maddening to know that you've made a note on an issue, but because you did not put it in the right place, it does you no good. It can also be quite disconcerting when you see a note in your own handwriting years (or even months) after you wrote it and you don't have a clue what it means.

If you want to note information that you (or someone else) will need later, it should be in a memo to the file. Such memos should be filed in the correspondence file, as well as in any relevant subfolder. If the note only needs to be temporary, you can write it on a post-it note, placing it on the cover of the relevant document or flagging the area of concern, sticking out of the file.

Make sure your note includes all needed information—what, why, who, where and when:

- "Document production, second wave may also include the warehouse downtown; see letter from A. M. Gilman to Frederick C. Murray, dated July 26, 1991," initialed **and** dated, stuck to the front of the appropriate document or right on top of the file in order to be seen immediately.

- "Attached is controlled group schedule from 1992 auditor's letter; compare at next IRS filing," initialed **and** dated, attached to a copy of that schedule, and clipped on left side of the plan folder on top of the last IRS filing.

As you are writing the note, keep in mind that people reading the note later (including you) will not remember or be as familiar with the situation or the documents as you are now. After all, that is why you are writing the note.

If You Cannot Finish the Project, Write a Memo

With any luck, you will soon find yourself juggling a number of assignments for different lawyers. As a result, you will be interrupted or delayed in the progress of one or another of your projects. If you find yourself spending a substantial amount of time "reviewing project status," that is, updating yourself on where the project stands, consider developing shorthand reminders, just to reorient yourself.

- Keep detailed notes, or checklists of your progress to date, and the steps that remain to be finished.

- Dictate a quick memo of what has been completed—and especially what remains to be done, noting any deadlines—as soon as you finish part of an assignment, while you still remember it. It is **much** easier to review a memo than a whole file, six months of correspondence, or your working papers and drafts to pick up the threads of where you left off.

- Always put a reminder in your computer or on your calendar to check back on assignments still in progress.

■ If events have been dragging on for some time, discuss with the lawyer whether it would be useful to write a letter reminding everyone where the project stands, to try to get things off the back burner.

Do Not Set Up Your Own Case Files or Let Documents Go Unfiled

Documents relevant to a case or client should be filed by your secretary as soon as possible in the main client files so everyone has access to them. This includes any memos the lawyer may have written to you, along with the originals of letters and other documents mailed to you. This is not just a recommendation: **this is the rule**.

Anytime you (or anyone else, including senior lawyers), hoard unfiled originals of documents, you waste your time and everyone else's for no purpose. Weeks, months, or even years from now, you will forget you have the original documents, others may never know you have them, everyone will spend time looking for them, and the same documents may have to be requested repeatedly from the client. Such waste is unconscionable in this efficiency-driven economy. Clients will not pay for it, nor will your co-workers stand for it.

Client or case files are designed so that many people can easily find what they need. Don't second-guess the system by trying to invent one of your own. For example, do not set up a separate file of all the correspondence that was mailed to you, apart from the main correspondence file. Do not set up parallel files of papers that are relevant only to your part of the project (i.e., memos the lawyer wrote to you, carbon copies of letters other people sent, your drafts, the lawyer's markups of your work, etc.).

You will confuse your secretary into thinking that yours is the "real" file, and no one (including you) will ever really know whether anything important got filed in there by accident. If a file looks like the main client file, it will be assumed to be the client file. If it is not, that wastes time.

You can—and should—keep **copies** of materials that are relevant only to you (your drafts, working copies of documents, carbon copies of letters, etc.), in your office or filing cabinets. But you should realize, and make sure your secretary knows, that these are just for your comfort and convenience. These are strictly **temporary working files** and should be labeled as such.

Temporary, convenience files should contain only duplicate or superseded materials that you would throw away but for the possibility that they might help you remember where you are in a project or in case questions arise. They should contain only those documents or notes that would be meaningless to anyone else. These documents are the ones you keep only for your own peace of mind and/or because of your irrepressible pack-rat instincts.

Any of your working papers that are relevant, such as notes detailing a phone call of a client's changes on a document, should be filed with the regular correspondence or working papers. Perhaps you can set up a separate section in the main set of files labeled as your working papers pertaining to a specific project. But **all** legal research documents and memoranda should be put in the client file, not your own personal subject file.

Even worse than setting up a separate system is having no system at all. You do not want to leave the person who works with you or who picks up where you left off with piles of unsorted papers, draft after draft, with no indication of which is which, or what is final. Make sure the files are maintained as you go. You will find not only that this is easier on everyone else, especially your secretary, but that it makes work easier for you too.

Make Sure Computer Documents Are Filed

The advent of computers has made the chore of filing and organizing paper worse, not easier. The short-term benefits of computerized mail and word processing at everyone's fingertips have not been accompanied by a long-term ability to organize those new information products. Accurate filing is made even more difficult because often a secretary never even sees the final document. You can no longer be prevented from making big mistakes by a great secretary who organizes your work product if he does not have access to it.

This concern is not about mistakes of substance, but about mistakes of time and memory, efficiency and productivity. These problems are insidious because they are not obvious and their accretion takes time to have an effect.

You can go for a long time without realizing how bad your files are, and then it is often too late, because:

- documents (especially electronic mail messages) have been deleted to conserve memory in the computer;

- you forgot how you named a document, so you can't retrieve it;

- you have several versions of the same document which you can no longer differentiate without spending too much time; or

- the computer has crashed.

A worst-case scenario: documents are sent back and forth electronically, different people make changes, everyone has a different marked-up version in their own working files, nothing but the cover letter shows up in the permanent file, and the client calls to ask which of the three documents you sent is the final one. Not only do you have **no idea** how to answer that question ("uh, the one we sent you last?"), you have no idea how to tell which version in your own computer system is current. The most horrible (and not at all unlikely) answer is that the final document is really a blend: the partner's version has that new paragraph in article two that the client called about, but the other lawyer working on the document has the latest limitations article, while only the paralegal's version contains the latest round of corrections.

It is imperative that you develop working habits which recognize this fundamental problem in office procedure. This edict cannot be stressed enough. By taking advantage of the ease of using computers to create and modify documents, usually no one person is in complete control of the paper flow. This can result in having to conduct fruitless and wasteful searches for things that someone "knows he did" but of which there is no record.

It is so easy to send off an electronic mail message and think the matter resolved. (It certainly feels resolved!) But let me assure you: the matter is not resolved until a copy of that message finds its way into the client file. One way to ensure that this happens is to "carbon copy" your secretary on the mail message, instructing him to put it in the file. In most computer systems, you are the only one who can do this. Until you include your secretary in the electronic "paper trail," you can never be as effective or productive.

Make Sure Key Drafts Are Filed

"Key drafts" are those draft documents sent to the client for review, those sent to an overly busy partner for approval, or any other significant draft that seems to be taking more than a week or two to complete. It is not necessary to file on Tuesday a draft that you know will be finalized by Thursday, or drafts that you know the lawyer will edit within a day or two. But do label all key drafts and keep them in order in the file.

Do not wait until every "i" is dotted and every "t" crossed to file draft documents because that may never happen. Drafts might not be finalized for a long time, and you may need to refresh your memory in the meantime so you can pick up the loose ends. You may think you'll never forget where you were on each and every painful project, but you will.

Filing key drafts away—as opposed to leaving them stacked in piles on your desk—has strong advantages. The following example illustrates this rule very well.

A partner had an unexpected meeting with the client. Normally, he would call the associate on the case and get an update, or the associate would go to the meeting herself. However, the associate was on vacation and, as luck would have it, so was the paralegal. Naturally enough, even though the paralegal and the associate handle all the day-to-day work, the partner wanted to review the files to find out where things stood so he would be knowledgeable about the client's affairs. The last thing in the file was the IRS's request for information, with a required response date that was long past.

All the partner could find in the associate's office were three generations of the paralegal's drafts for the reply, along with undated and indecipherable notes written by the paralegal, like: "I'll stop by later on this." Fur flew upon the paralegal's return. Although this person had a most reasonable and logical explanation, that did little to make up for the trouble that was caused. As proof, I have a vivid recollection of the partner's anger, but I'll be darned if I can recall that paralegal's explanation, although I do remember it made perfect sense at the time.

You may think that, in this example, it was up to the associate to keep things straight, or that this was the associate's fault. Wrong. Picture the partner walking into your office and asking for this file. This may help you realize the need to keep the file organized.

Save Certain Drafts

Keep on file certain drafts of major documents, not just until they are done but sometimes as long as a year or two. It is amazing how often people decide they want to go back a step, or want to know the difference between this version and that, or want those last changes to be reflected in other documents as well. And these decisions do not always occur right away. It is much easier to have the documents to refer back to, instead of being forced to rely on memory or trying to reconstruct long-ago events.

It is **not** necessary to save every draft. You rarely need to keep all the versions it took for you to get from your first effort to the final document you gave the lawyer for review. However, in some special circumstances, you may need a record of the successive changes that the lawyer made incorporated into one document. Have your secretary mark up an original draft with all the changes made by the lawyer, even though the edits occurred at different times. This provides a paper trail of the issues that were considered in revising the document. Usually the more important changes, however, are those made by the client or those resulting from last-minute brainstorming sessions.

You will want to flag the few drafts you decide to save by putting them in a separate, temporary folder. Indicate a file destruction date, to minimize the firm's storage costs. Also, make sure to put a detailed label on the draft documents so it will be apparent what they are and why they were saved. An astounding amount of unnecessary paper is saved because no one has time to reevaluate the continuing usefulness of documents (or files) under changing circumstances. Correct labelling makes future review easy.

Do Not Throw Things Away

As with aphorisms like "out of sight, out of mind" and "absence makes the heart grow fonder," many pieces of advice have exact opposites. The previous rule states: Do not save all the drafts. Yet, here I say: Do not take it upon yourself to throw things away, especially when you are new at the job.

If you are a "pitcher" and not a "saver" (you too would have tossed the kids' old baseball cards, just like your mom or grandmother did), it may be difficult to realize that lawyers are totally dependent upon their documents, no matter how old and wrinkly they look or how irrelevant they seem. Sooner or later an attorney will come looking for something, and if you can honestly say "I never throw anything away," you are better off than if you have to reply, "Gee, that didn't look important to me."

For example, take a pension plan dated 1958. You may think, "This old one keeps falling out of the file, it's hard to read and there are four later versions in the file; surely they don't need this old one." Wrong. There is always an employee with 40 years' tenure at the company who quit and has never been heard from since, but who now has a hungry lawyer. Within two days after you finally throw something away, you will need it.

Of course, be reasonable here. The point is not to keep every draft or note (although some disorganized lawyers do inordinately value their scribbles on scraps of paper), but to keep only the important ones. Unfortunately, it's hard to always know the full significance of every document, and especially possible significance over time. It helps to ask those around you. It also helps to be an organized pack rat. It's wonderful to be able to resurrect a 14-year-old gem that resolves a question but is no longer in the reference materials because it was only the preamble to a ruling and not the ruling itself, all because you know exactly what is in your organized, clearly labeled files.

WORKING ON SPECIFIC KINDS OF PROJECTS

Legal Research

Like other projects, legal research requires a strategy. Ask the assigning attorney where he or she would start. Figure out where you will need to look ahead of time, and confirm that you are checking all the right sources in the right order. Consult the law librarians. They will usually be quite pleased to help and can show you many shortcuts.

When you conduct legal research, especially if you are new at it or do not do it very often, take notes of what you are doing and where you are looking, such as the name of the book and the date of the pocket part. Jot down the names of the cases you are reading and note why you think they are relevant or irrelevant.

If you are conducting legal research using computer databases, make notes of (or print out) your search requests as you go. These should show the libraries and files you chose for searching, as well as the search terms and their configuration that you used, along with the number of documents that were retrieved. Another good habit is to print out the table of citations for retrieved cases; you can then flag the most likely cases while you scan through the key words.

The reward of taking a little extra time here is saving time later. If you are interrupted, or you finish but are called back to work on that matter further, you do not have to spend time retracing your steps. Also, you need to be able to give a summary of what you accomplished to the lawyer so she can verify that you did all that was required. You want to be able to confidently field any questions about what sources you used and why you reached your conclusions.

There's another reason to document your work procedure while conducting legal research. When you present your results to the lawyer, you will be surprised how often it turns out that the question wasn't exactly what you thought it was. There may be a further issue that the lawyer is now interested in, which was not clear to either of you at the outset. Frequently, the precise language, issue or holding you are looking for is not there. It is easy to determine when a case is directly on point. The trouble is, most are not, and you will have to explain to the lawyer where you looked and why those cases you did find are (or are not) relevant. You do not want to have to reread all those cases.

Ongoing Projects with Third Parties

When working with third parties, scrupulously keep notes of every telephone conversation, no matter how trivial and commonplace it seems, and send follow up letters restating your understandings and assumptions. Spell everything out, even the things you think everyone in the field knows.

This is the trap: you understand what the insurance company representative says, for example, to be perfectly reasonable, and you think they understand the things you say in response. But three months later, after decisions have been made and steps taken, you discover that the insurance company did something that does not match at all what you thought was going to happen. You call and find out the representative has no recollection of the conversations, understandings and assumptions you thought you both shared. Indeed, the company has a totally different interpretation. Be careful not to take conversations at face value. If you do, you are presenting the other parties to conversations a chance to rewrite history.

Even taking great care to memorialize conversations might not save you from time-consuming backtracking, redoing work, delays, frustration and confusion, not to mention high legal fees for your client. The problem is that while it seems like you are speaking the same language, you really aren't. For example, insurance companies often use common words with new definitions only they know, and technical words that they define differently from everyone else in the field. Since they are using all the same words you are, you can be lulled into thinking that you are communicating on the same wavelength.

For many people you work with, clients and their employees, and even the government (although less so recently), you can more or less rely on common understandings and common sense. What they say is what they do, barring common misunderstandings that you can learn to avoid, or that you can at least correct, with their cooperation, once you discover the problem. This is not the case with everyone, however. Think of this possibility when you work with some insurance companies, consultants and lawyers outside your office. Not everyone's interest is the same as your own.

6

When You Return the Assignment

You always want to create the impression that your finished assignment is accurate and complete, in order to build the lawyer's trust in your work. One way to do this is to turn in projects with a polished appearance.

GIVE YOUR WORK ONE FINAL CHECK

Carefully review your work, as well as the work of others (such as copies produced by the copy center). You should also double-check the materials returned to you by the client. Add your own specific items to the following generic checklist:

■ Did you thoroughly check the subsequent history of the cases?

■ Did you research the most current rulings?

■ Did the secretary or the client follow the instructions on the form?

■ Did you use the final regulations just issued or the most recent version of the court rules?

■ Are the forms current?

■ Are all the dates filled in?

■ Are the documents signed?

■ Are the documents final?

Remember to double-check all specific tasks related to the project, even if you think the attorney in charge will also be checking. Since you accepted the assignment, it's primarily your responsibility.

REMIND IN WRITING

Give people notes and written reminders in addition to verbal reminders. Just because you mention something once does not mean the lawyer will remember.

For example, if you are returning a document with a deadline to a lawyer for review, do not just put the folder in the lawyer's office and assume she is aware of the deadline. At the very least, leave some papers on top from which the lawyer can glean the deadline. Better yet, put a note on the file saying "Settlement agreement deadline Friday, June 5, but client is going on vacation and must sign by Tuesday, June 2."

COMMUNICATE YOUR ASSUMPTIONS

You need to advise the lawyer about any assumptions you may have made in the course of completing an assignment. What follows is an example of the assumptions you might make while working on a project. The benefits of communicating these assumptions to the lawyer are also detailed.

Pension plans have "plan years" just as corporations have fiscal years. You are asked to "change the plan year." You think, "What about the limitation year?" since you know that the IRS requires some plans to define the year on which certain government limitations are based. After checking the plan, you see that the limitation year is defined simply as the "plan year," without a specific date, so you decide that this section of the plan does not have to be amended.

The lawyer needs to know that you thought about, researched and dismissed the need to amend that section concerning the plan's limitation year. Returning the assignment without any reference to the limitation year is not as helpful as giving back that assignment with a checklist that includes the following notation: "Limitation year—defined as plan year (plan § 1.15, p. 4). Assume no change required."

You can derive several benefits for taking care to communicate your assumptions:

- You get credit for thinking about additional issues that occurred to you.

- The lawyer gets a chance to correct your assumptions because you have called attention to them. Your training is furthered by the attorney explaining how the issue you raised is (or is not) relevant in this case.

- Stating your assumptions may remind the lawyer that one of the issues you raised was forgotten, so it can be applied to other, similar projects. (This is an ongoing educational process for all of us.)

- Your list of assumptions makes it easier for the lawyer to see what you did not consider, providing an opportunity for further training.

GIVE LAWYERS THE WHOLE PROJECT

Turn in a completed project for the attorney to review, not just the pieces. It takes a great deal of energy, and some changing of gears, for a lawyer to quit working on his or her own projects to review yours. And needing to review a project twice wastes the lawyer's time. Make it easier by minimizing the number of interruptions.

It may be perfectly clear to you how the one missing piece of the project does not affect the rest, but seeing only part will surely raise questions in the lawyer's mind about the other parts. Providing the whole package will allow the lawyer to answer those questions.

Waiting to give the lawyer the whole project also allows you to refine and correct the earlier pieces while completing the rest of the assignment. As you finish each aspect of a project, you naturally think it is complete, and in the best form it could be. As you continue to work, however, you may discover a new issue that must be addressed, or find ways to improve those pieces you completed earlier. In addition, you may realize that changes are necessary in order to make the whole project fit together.

While there are some good reasons for getting feedback from the lawyer part way through the assignment (for example, to make sure you are on track), in general, you do not want to embarrass yourself by having to retrieve a project to work on it further. This could undermine both your confidence and the lawyer's trust in you. Although the temptation to get immediate feedback on your efforts may be great, do not return part of the assignment just for that reason.

GIVE LAWYERS THE FINISHED PROJECT

Give the lawyer the finished project that is typed, corrected and reflects your best effort. Do **not** leave blanks to be filled in later or a last round of corrections to be made after the lawyer's changes. Leaving a few minor corrections for later is acceptable only when time does not permit you to wait for the project to be completely finished.

There are a couple of reasons for this. It is hard to review an unfinished project; it is natural (if sometimes unreasonable), for the reviewer to fear that he or she will have to review the project all over again later when it is finally done. It is hard to give your best effort to reviewing something which you know you will have to review again later. Also, if it appears that the project is unfinished, the lawyer will feel free to make all kinds of minor preference or stylistic changes which would not otherwise be necessary if other changes were not being made at the same time.

You always want to create the impression that your finished assignment is accurate and complete, in order to build the lawyer's trust in your work. One way to do this is to turn in projects with a polished appearance. This requires taking time to proofread. While you may drive your secretary crazy, it is necessary.

This is all part of the larger philosophy that appearance matters: if it **looks** good, it will be presumed to **be** good. It is best to create the illusion that you rarely make mistakes by keeping your corrections to yourself.

GIVE LAWYERS EVERYTHING NECESSARY FOR REVIEW

When you give the lawyer your work to review, also include all the related papers needed to accomplish an accurate review, such as the lawyer's marked-up draft (which shows the attorney's suggested changes), the appropriate file, and the relevant correspondence from the client. You want to make this as simple for the lawyer as possible.

Never throw away the lawyer's markup of corrections and suggested changes, even if you're sure they have all been made. Seeing this markup again will help remind the lawyer what he or she was thinking about when the original suggestions were made; it will provide reassurance that all the required changes have in fact been made; and it may even provide evidence that the lawyer actually did forget to tell you something. You should also keep a copy of this markup to remind yourself of that attorney's preferences when the time comes to do a similar project.

DO NOT WAIT UNTIL THE DEADLINE TO TURN IN YOUR WORK

Even if you are convinced your work is perfect, give the finished project to the lawyer **well before** the deadline in case changes are necessary. At the very least, the attorney will probably edit your writing. However, it may turn out that you need to gather further information. You want to avoid any potential crisis by leaving enough time to take care of the unexpected.

ACCOMMODATE LAWYERS' WEAKNESSES

If the lawyer is disorganized or known for losing things, do **not** give him or her your only copy of any document, the original of your work, or the last set of the client's papers. In general, it is not wise to let go of the last copy of any materials you are currently working on. When the lawyer calls you with a question, it makes a good impression if you can turn to the same page of the document and promptly give the answer.

7

After the Project Is Done

Keep track of the outcome of the projects you have worked on by inquiring about their status after your part is done. Following up maximizes the possibility for getting the training and review of your work that everyone needs to progress.

MAKE SURE IT GETS FILED

Make sure your secretary accurately files everything, **especially** the final, executed copies. Your work is useless if no one can find it later. Training your secretary to file accurately and in a timely manner is critical.

Also make sure the drafts of documents are filed even if you don't know the final outcome. You secretary must know, however, to remove the drafts when the final copies come in. It is human nature to pile documents on top of others without checking to see their relationship to the whole file.

MAKE SURE IT'S REALLY DONE

If the lawyer does not get back to you on a project, find ways to follow up on its status, such as enlisting the help of the attorney's secretary. For example, if you have electronically mailed your draft to the lawyer, ask the lawyer's secretary to mail you back the final version. This means you will have an accurate sample to use in the future, and you can see what changes the lawyer made in your work.

When you've sent the lawyer a draft document for review but you have not heard anything further, follow up after allowing a reasonable time. Choose a time when you suspect the lawyer will be able to work on the project, like Saturday morning or at 6:30 on a weekday. Lawyers always love to see you working extra hours, and that may motivate them to deal with your project.

Keep track of the outcome of the projects you have worked on by inquiring about their status after your part is done. Following up maximizes the possibility for getting the training and review of your work that everyone needs to progress.

FOLLOW THE PROJECT THROUGH ON THE DEADLINE DATE

Assuming the deadline is a **real** deadline, and not just the day the lawyer would like the documents to go out, stay around to make sure the documents actually get out that day. Do **not** just park the final draft on the lawyer's desk and go home at 6:00. If it is getting late, work with your secretary to make sure the project is all ready to go out and printed on letterhead, with all the enclosures, envelopes and certified mailing slips finished.

If the lawyer is away from the office, it will be up to you to stay late in order to take care of any last minute corrections or details. Even though you were careful to warn the lawyer ahead of time about the need to finalize or review a document before it goes out, chances are she will get tied up on some other rush project and forget about yours. It is **your responsibility** to see your project through to the end.

WHAT COMES NEXT?

You will want to iron out with the lawyer exactly what follow-up details you are responsible for. Although I have listed this rule near the end, as a practical matter, this is an issue you will want to clarify early on as part of your working relationship with the lawyer.

Follow up is often difficult, since it is the lawyer who will end up with the final outcome or documents. If you have a good working relationship with the attorney's secretary, you can ask him or her to run things by you for a final check. This way, you will know that the details were completed, and completed accurately.

SOLICIT AND ACCEPT FURTHER TRAINING

Don't wait for lawyers to offer to train you because they never will. "On-the-job training" may suggest to you that someone you work with will take time to explain things to you. Not so. It means that **you** have the opportunity to turn your assignments into learning experiences by finding out and understanding the reasons for the lawyer's changes in your work.

It takes practice before your work will go through a lawyer's review without change. With some projects, that may never happen, especially if your task is to get the first workable draft on paper. Getting the concepts in order, providing a workable structure, and ensuring that the facts are recorded accurately, may be all that is required.

Actively solicit periodic feedback on your work. No one likes to tell you bad news, and if the only comments concerning your work are good, everyone will assume you know this already. In either case, it is important for you to get feedback if you are to progress.

Do not assume that just because no one is saying anything, there is nothing to say. And don't dismiss seemingly offhand comments— these may be all the feedback you receive, and they may indicate problems. Do not overreact to such comments, but find out what they mean.

Listen to criticism without defensiveness. Realize that some criticism may come from the lawyer's unreasonable expectation that you can read his or her mind. However, there may be aspects of your performance that you must change, at least to work with that lawyer. Try to objectively sort out which is which.

Politely listen to the lawyer's comments about what he or she thinks is wrong with your work, even if you think these comments are picky and irrelevant. You may feel wronged at the moment, but upon further reflection, you might decide they were right. You do not want to close the door on hearing more. If lawyers feel that you will accept their comments positively, they will feel freer to give you more feedback, both good and bad. Accept any petty preferences graciously, realizing that this is the attorneys' ball game; be assured that they never forget that fact.

Make it clear that you understand that every mistake is significant. It may be trivial in the larger world, forgotten in the long run, but it is very important in terms of lawyers' developing trust in you. How you handle hearing about the mistake is something they will remember, probably longer than the mistake itself. Most lawyers need many positive experiences with your work to offset a negative one. Make your response to criticism a positive experience instead of another negative one.

Also make clear your intention to correct the problem in the future, and point out your own provisions to follow through with that intention. As the saying goes, you can make all the mistakes you want, just don't make the same ones twice.

Counting the Minutes:

The Essential Training Guide for Time & Billing Techniques

by Dana L. Graves

This monograph is dedicated to all those beleaguered legal secretaries who are responsible for the onerous chore of inputing time sheets for attorneys and legal assistants, some of whom don't always cooperate in the effort.

The recession merely hastened a process that began several years ago when corporations started expanding their legal departments. Enhanced in-house expertise resulted in a more sophisticated clientele, able to read the billing sheet with a discerning eye.

Evans, "Upcoming Year Likely to Bring More of the Same," *California Law Business*, 24 (Daily Journal Corporation, Oct. 28, 1991)

Introduction

My, how times have changed. From the fast-growing, economic-booming, almost-anything-goes '80s, we've now arrived at the decade of the '90s, where the new buzzwords for law firms are "efficiency," "cost effectiveness" and "client service." Far from worrying about how to find and hire the additional people necessary to staff all the work pouring in, law firms are now concerned with the real possibilities of losing existing business to more competitive firms. Because of the recession, and downturn of real estate and corporate business, firms also need to win over new clients to replace reduced work from existing clients.

This monograph addresses only one issue, but that issue—ethical, efficient and effective time billing practices—is one which all law firm clients are now closely examining. It is also the one area which has been under closer scrutiny for some time, and significantly, the area where firms can be more competitive and innovative, thus winning over clients, while at the same time maintaining revenues.

This monograph is a quick, but comprehensive, tool for developing profitable timekeeping habits. It will:

- introduce new staff members to the concept and purpose of time billing;

- show them how to capture all their time, how to word time descriptions appropriately, and how **not** to describe time;

- detail the importance of working within firm and client billing policies, with examples to work through policy questions;

- show them the mechanics of keeping track of time worked;

- inform them of the importance of meeting annual billable hours requirements; and

- review each person's responsibilities as a timekeeper.

Everyone should now recognize that the days of presenting two-line bills—"Fee for services rendered, May 1987: $125,000"— are long past. But complying with client strictures on billing, while at the same time developing cost-effective, efficient practices—all **without** spending hours of administrative time on training—has not always been possible or easy.

Until now.

We're striving to get the lowest level of competent associate working on our matters, and have seen a decline in the average hourly rate we pay outside counsel. You don't need a Rolls Royce to go to the store.

Hal M. Hofherr, General Counsel, General Dynamics (San Diego).

I have always audited bills because with predictable regularity I find something that I question, like two lawyers billing us for a conference where one charges us half an hour and the other an hour.

Thomas J. Bauch, Senior Vice President/General Counsel, Levi Strauss & Company (San Francisco).

Both quoted in Nance-Nash, "10 General Counsel Tell How They Control Fees," *California Law Business*, 18 (Daily Journal Corporation, Jan. 27, 1992).

1

The New Reality of the Law Practice

It used to be that lawyers and other timekeepers could bill their time by simply estimating the number of hours worked for a particular client, and describing, in broad terms, the type of work performed. Bills simply worded "Fees for legal services rendered, May 1987—$125,000" were not at all uncommon. Because detailed, accurate and descriptive timekeeping can be a somewhat onerous task, this approach worked well for some time. "Ball parking time" was considered an appropriate substitute for keeping detailed time charts. (*See* "Fee Case Shows Fast-Lane Billing," *The National Law Journal*, 3 (Jan. 13, 1992)).

But those days are gone. In fact, along with clients' increasing sophistication and scrutiny, a brand new service business has developed for the sole purpose of auditing legal bills for corporations.

This new reality means—for some experienced lawyers—learning how to keep appropriate time records for the first time. It also means that all new staff who bill time must develop efficient timekeeping habits right away, in order to capture all their billable time, and avoid later write offs.

IMPORTANCE OF ETHICAL, EFFICIENT AND EFFECTIVE TIME BILLING

Timekeepers experience pressure from a variety of sources. They are pressured to complete difficult assignments in short periods of time. They are also pressured to compete with their peers, both in terms of performance, and with respect to billable hours.

Because timekeeping is sometimes a matter of making judgment calls—for example, do you bill for your time to proofread a five-page letter to a client when you're training a new secretary, a letter you may not have needed to proofread if you had an experienced secretary?—and because timekeeping is a laborious task, new timekeepers sometimes take shortcuts. They simply estimate the time spent on particular client matters, and provide only the most general time descriptions.

This is no longer appropriate, nor is it tolerated by most clients. Since what law firms sell is their services, provided in packages of total time spent, that **"product" must be perceived by the customer as time well spent.** Clients will no longer give legal work to firms where they feel this is not the case. In fact, if the problem is an extreme one, clients will sue firms for abusive billing practices.

Clients are also sensitive to the issues of overstaffing, not delegating work to the lowest appropriate person, and generally inefficient work habits. These efficiency issues may, for the most part, be outside the influence of individual timekeepers. However, you can make sure that your own work is efficient, that you work within the guidelines set for each assignment, and that you keep the ultimate cost of your work in mind.

Time descriptions are somewhat akin to the labels on products in grocery stores. When you pick up a package of wheat bread, you probably look for the ingredients, and if the package label shows ingredients you're trying to avoid, you won't buy that bread. Think of the "consumer" of your time—the firm's client—when drafting descriptions of your time. The person reviewing the bills must be convinced that this is something he or she wants to pay for. If your time descriptions are sufficiently detailed, and do not violate any specific billing rules established by the client, your time will generally be perceived as time well spent.

DEFINITIONS OF HOURLY, CONTINGENCY, VALUE BILLING & FLAT FEES

Hourly Billing. Billing clients for each hour of work performed has been the traditional method for charging for legal services, at least for the last 40 years or so. Time sheets are used to record the amount of time spent working for a client, in addition to describing the work performed. All hourly systems have in common the fact that the time spent working is the "package" billed to the client.

Hourly billing means not only billing for the amount of time spent on performing legal services, it also means breaking each hour into blocks of time. This allows the timekeeper to bill for partial hours. A number of variations in billing increments exist:

- every fifteen minutes, called the quarter-hour system
- every ten minutes, called the sixth-of-an-hour system
- every six minutes, called the tenth-of-an-hour system

Hypothetically, in an eight-hour working day, you will have 80 six-minute segments, 48 ten-minute segments, or 32 fifteen-minute segments of time to bill.

The minimum information required to allocate the time properly includes:

- noting the client and matter numbers,
- the total time spent on a particular task,
- the date the work was performed, and
- a description of the work performed, for example:
  Reviewed plaintiff's second request for production of documents in Jones v. Smith; prepared notes for responses.

Considering the above requirements, you can see that hourly timekeeping itself takes time. If you record your time contemporaneously with the work performed, and keep your time records current **every** day, you will reduce the burden of this task. Reconstructing an entire month of time sheets is no fun. You will also most likely miss significant periods of billable time if much time passes between when the work was performed and when it was billed.

Contingency Billing. In contingency fee cases—which are usually plaintiff personal injury, torts and collections matters—the firm agrees that its legal fees will be paid from the proceeds of the case. The client pays legal fees only if and when the lawyer has obtained a recovery for the client. That is, gaining payment of legal fees is "contingent" upon the attorney winning or settling the case, with a monetary recovery for the client.

Contingency percentages ordinarily range from twenty-five to thirty-three percent of the recovery, if any, achieved through settlement without going to trial. The percentage amount typically increases to forty or fifty percent of the jury or court award if the matter must be tried.

In contingent fee cases, the firm is predicting that it will win the case for the client, and that the amount of its percentage recovery will exceed what it would have billed at an hourly rate. Of course, the benefit to the client is that no legal fees are due if the firm achieves no settlement or award. However, it's important to note that the costs of the litigation—filing fees, photocopying costs, postage, etc.—must still be paid by the client, even if no monetary recovery is ever achieved.

Even though in contingency cases the client will not be billed for hourly services, this does not mean that timekeepers escape the hassle of time records. There are a number of reasons for keeping track of time worked in contingency cases: for example, a conflict with the client may arise, or the firm might want to track whether time spent working on certain matters is profitable. And, of course, there is always the annual billable hours requirement to be met. (*See* discussion of billable hour requirements in **Chapter Nine**.)

Value Billing. A relatively new concept is "value billing." When a client has agreed to pay for the **result** of legal services, the firm bills for the value of those services. The price is set by what the legal service seems to be worth to the client. For example:

> One firm was willing to be billed at 60 percent of their normal rate if they lost a very complex case involving serious legal issues, but if we won they would get 140 percent of their normal rate.

Edward A. Cutter, Vice President/ General Counsel/Secretary, The Clorox Company (Oakland), quoted in Nance-Nash, "10 General Counsel Tell How They Control Fees," *California Law Business*, 18 (Daily Journal Corporation, Jan. 27, 1992).

This type of approach to billing has been somewhat difficult to implement, although there are several good reasons for trying. As pointed out by Altman and Weil, noted authors on law office management:

> [H]ourly billing ignores the true value of a lawyer's services.... [E]xpertise, proficiency, and productivity in the performance of work are negatively rewarded by hourly billing.

Value billing is much easier to discuss than accomplish because of the wide acceptance of hourly billing, and the difficulty inherent in using subjective factors such as those listed above to set fees.

Flat Fee or Fixed Rate Billing. Other firms have adopted equally innovative billing strategies, for example, fixing fees at flat rates for services like lease negotiations, corporate formations, or other fairly repetitive services. For clients, the primary advantage of flat fee billing is that they know in advance what the work will cost: there are no surprises when the bill is received.

> On certain routine transactions . . . we are estimating the amount of hours the work should take and capping the fee on that transaction. If we think it should only take 100 hours then that's all we'll pay, unless there are extenuating circumstances. Outside counsel is in the business of billing hours; in-house attorneys' goal is to accomplish tasks. Caps move you closer to accomplishing tasks, not billing hours.

Ibid., quoting Jan Charles Gray, Senior Vice President/General Counsel/Secretary, Ralphs Grocery Company (Los Angeles).

A variation of flat or fixed fees is "item charges." In this type of billing structure, a firm charges for each item involved in the representation of the client. Common item charges for litigation attorneys may include opening the file, preparing a motion, attending a deposition, or making an appearance in court.

OVERVIEW OF TIME BILLING PROCESS

Keeping close track of hours worked by attorneys, legal assistants and other timekeepers makes sense, even for contingency, value billing and flat fee arrangements. In addition to billing for hourly time, firms must know how much time is being put into what types of matters, and for which clients, for a number of reasons:

- determining the cost of the firm's services
- determining the value of the work in progress
- aiding the supervision process
- allowing coordination and control of staffing
- tracking both the profitable and not-so-profitable areas of practice

Therefore, every lawyer and legal assistant should understand the process of how timekeeping is accomplished.

Many different forms of time sheets exist. But they all have one purpose—to provide a uniform method and structure for recording client billable and administrative time. All time worked in one day should be recorded either directly on the time sheet, or on your calendar, daily appointment chart or even in notes on a legal pad. Ultimately, however, unless you input your time directly into your firm's computer system, the amount of time worked, along with the client and matter numbers or codes, and a description of the work performed, must be recorded on the documents required by the firm.

Most firms prefer that their timekeepers submit their time sheets for inputing on **at least** a weekly basis. Regular submission of time sheets is important for a number of reasons. If you delay writing your time down, you might forget portions of the work you performed. Also, the people who input time sheets into the computer need to have sufficient time to handle this responsibility. Waiting until the end of the month—or other cut-off time—can mean that time sheets for that month won't be included in the month's client bills.

In some firms, lawyers and legal assistants input their own time sheets. This is usually the most efficient method, because it combines two steps—recording and inputing time—into just one. But attorneys and legal assistants don't always have sufficient knowledge of how to work with time billing software, may not want to handle their time responsibilities in this manner, or simply (and most often), just don't have the time available.

When not handled directly by the timekeeper, time sheet inputing can either be assigned to a specific billing department, or handled by the timekeeper's secretary. In the former situation, the persons responsible for time sheet handling will input the information on the time sheet **exactly** as it appears, poor handwriting, incorrect billing numbers and all. If possible, print your time descriptions and client/matter numbers. Unless the information you provide is clearly readable, there is a good chance it will be misinterpreted, and incorrect information will be entered into the computer.

On the other hand, if your secretary is handling the input, he or she may be able to fill in missing information, or read illegible handwriting. Either way, however, you should **always** review the draft billing information input from your time sheets. This will help ensure that the proper client and matter numbers were recorded, and that the description contains no typographical errors.

After you have confirmed that the input time records are correct, or any problems fixed, the time can be further processed. At the end of each month (sometimes quarterly instead of monthly), the billing department will put together all time for each client, separated into individual matters, and prepare a draft bill for review by the billing attorney. This draft bill is sometimes called a "prebill" invoice.

The billing attorney is the attorney designated to review all of the bills for a particular client before the bills are sent out. This attorney checks the prebills to determine:

- that the time has been properly allocated to this client,
- that the time descriptions are appropriate, and

■ if any adjustments in the bill should be made.

If the billing attorney determines that too much time was expended on a particular matter—or that an adjustment in the bill must be made for other reasons—the time will be either "written down" (reduced) or "written off" (deleted). There are several reasons either of these steps can be taken.

The attorney may feel that the persons performing the work did not work very efficiently, or the time descriptions do not justify the time recorded. In these cases, the individual timekeeper's work habits or poor timekeeping caused a reduction in the bill.

Some write-downs occur simply because the billing attorney feels that client will object to the size of the bill. It's also possible that this particular client may have strict guidelines about not being billed for certain tasks. These types of reductions are, of course, not the fault of the timekeepers. But it is incumbent upon you to determine—**ahead of time**—if clients have specific billing requirements or restrictions, so you can avoid this problem.

Once any adjustments to the prebill required by the billing attorney are made, the final bill is prepared and sent to the client for payment. The amount and level of detail provided on the client's bill varies from firm to firm. Usually, however, the minimum information provided includes:

■ names (or initials) of all timekeepers, along with their billing rates
■ the dates on which work was performed
■ the increment of time worked on each date, by whom, and a description of the work performed
■ all charges for expense items, such as photocopying, facsimile transmissions, overtime and messenger bills

In the past, clients simply paid the bills they were presented without question. But now, clients scrutinize law firm bills closely. The client's representative will be looking for ways to reduce charges for incorrectly allocated time, unauthorized expenses, overstaffing, and other inappropriate billings. Timekeepers must make sure that their time entries survive the review by the client as well as that performed by the billing partner.

As law firms grew in size and their practice became more diverse and faster-paced, . . . year-end billing system[s] became obsolete. The managing partners no longer knew what everyone was doing and no one knew the relative cost of the firm's various services. Efficiency experts pointed out that failing to record lawyer time was like failing to record the inventory of work in progress in a manufacturing plant. Lawyers were reminded of Abraham Lincoln's admonition that lawyers' time and advice was their stock in trade.

Geoffrey C. Hazard, "Ethics," *The National Law Journal*, 19 (Monday, Feb. 17, 1992) (from a column appearing monthly).

2

The Purposes for Tracking & Billing Time

TIME IS LEGAL SERVICES "PRODUCT" SOLD TO CLIENTS

Time sheets provide the financial backbone of law firms because most often, client billings are computed from the information contained in time sheets. While the client is paying for the legal services provided, those services must be quantified, and in hourly billing systems, the increments of time on bills constitutes the "product" sold to clients.

This does not mean, however, that the collection of time sheets should become an end in an of itself. As pointed out by Yale Law School Professor Hazard:

There is nothing inherently evil about time sheets. Along the way, however, a subtle change occurred: The time sheet—created as a control on "inventory"—now became the inventory itself. Law firms sold this inventory as lawyer time rather than selling the results as legal service. The important thing became, not "What did you do?," but "How much time did you spend?"

Geoffrey C. Hazard, "Ethics," *The National Law Journal*, 19 (Monday, Feb. 17, 1992) (from a column appearing monthly). When recording your time, always keep in mind that what you are billing for is **legal services rendered.**

HOURLY TIME SHEETS ARE USED TO KEEP TRACK OF PRODUCTIVITY

As noted by two of the premiere authorities on law firm management, "Those firms which have learned to manage the use of time carefully, and hence to use their people effectively, achieve both better client service and higher economic rewards." M. Altman & R. Weil, *How to Manage Your Law Office*, section 11.02 at 11-3 (rev. perm. ed. 1991). Time records give supervising attorneys a chance to review the work of junior attorneys and legal assistants. This allows them to check on the following:

- the progress of work on particular matters
- the variety of work performed, to ensure a wide exposure to the law practice
- that work is being performed efficiently
- that time descriptions meet the standards demanded by clients
- that each individual supervised is working productively

You can also use daily time records to keep track of your own productivity. If you keep track of where you've been, you can improve your efficiency, ensure you are exposed to a broad variety of projects, and in general, take control of your career. You will also find that the discipline of keeping time records allows you to focus on where you spend your time, and how well.

Perhaps you will spot areas where you can work more efficiently or where you need more experience. For example, regularly reviewing your time records can point out:

■ how often you are interrupted (this can be reflected by several short time entries)

■ if your projects are sufficiently varied to provide thorough training on a variety of tasks

■ whether your work on similar projects is getting more efficient because you are expending less time as you gain experience.

You will also most likely spot areas where you can improve your work habits. *See* **Chapter Seven,** "Time Management Tools," for advice about using your time more efficiently.

DETERMINE WHICH MATTERS/AREAS OF PRACTICE ARE PROFITABLE

All law firms are concerned, especially in these recessionary days, about which areas of the practice are truly profitable. Without keeping track of time spent in various practice areas, and tracking write-downs, write-offs, and finally, payments for the total time billed, firms would have no idea which areas were producing the highest revenue. Law firm accounting departments periodically produce reports showing revenues produced by different practice areas, by types of matters handled, and from billings to key clients. All this important management information would be much harder to amass absent detailed time records.

PROVIDE HISTORICAL INFORMATION ON WHICH TO BASE MANAGEMENT DECISIONS

Just as with any other business, law firm managers need to know where the firm has been in order to forecast where it will be in the future, and to establish plans for that future. For example, complete hourly time records can provide information on whether the firm should:

■ create a work product retrieval database in order to decrease nonbillable time spent looking for earlier briefs and legal memoranda

■ hire additional associates to handle expanding work for those clients for which increased billable hours were recorded

■ decrease its involvement in bar activities because too many nonbillable hours were allocated to that time code

■ explore the possibility of creating document clerk (or paralegal assistant) positions because time records for legal assistants reflect that most time spent numbering documents was written off

■ expand its investment in computers for all attorneys in order to decrease waiting time for work product turnaround from secretaries

■ install a document assembly software package that will cut down nonbillable time spent "cutting and pasting" corporate and real estate agreements

Of course, these decisions can be made in the absence of detailed time records. But without the data showing that these problems exist, the fact that there is a problem may not become apparent as quickly.

PROVIDE BASIS FOR COST ESTIMATES FOR CLIENTS

Most clients want to know—in advance—what the required legal services for a certain matter will cost them. This is true for divorces, tax filings, real estate purchases, contract negotiations and complex litigation cases. To provide this information for its clients, the law firm must know many specifics about the particular matter. For example, with litigation matters, attorneys must consider the complexity of the issues involved, the likely number of depositions that must be taken, the extent of discovery required, and what motions will most likely be filed, just to list a few.

But once this information is ascertained, the firm must look at its historical time records to estimate the cost of litigation, based upon the average amounts of time and costs involved in similar pieces of litigation. If clients start requesting flat-fee billing, having comprehensive time records available for research means the firm can meet this request, and at the same time, know that it will be charging appropriate amounts.

TIME RECORDS REQUIRED BY COURTS IN FEE AWARD SITUATIONS

In some cases, courts award fees to law firms. That is, courts are authorized in particular types of cases to order the opposing party (or, in bankruptcy cases, the bankrupt company or individual), to pay the legal fees and expenses of the winning party. Before a court will enter such an order, however, the firm asking for an award of fees must provide detailed records of the time expended on the case. Just like clients, courts have particular rules about what time will be reimbursed.

Exactly what courts require to award fees is beyond the scope of this monograph. But all timekeepers must keep in mind that not only will a billing attorney and client closely review all time entries, but these same entries may also be subjected to the scrutiny of a court.

In fairly rare circumstances, not only will courts award fees to the prevailing party, but a multiplier will be used to reward exceptional results or to reward firms for taking on unpopular cases. In such cases, courts can multiply the firm's hourly rates by a certain amount—a "multiplier"—and award that higher total. Obviously, the more hours the court approves for reimbursement, the higher the fee award.

In bankruptcy cases, applications for fee awards are particularly scrutinized by courts. Although the level of scrutiny may vary from court to court and from case to case, federal bankruptcy courts have the reputation for enforcing fairly strict rules for fee applications. A good example is the new billing guidelines which were recently drafted for the U.S. Trustee's Office in Los Angeles. These guidelines recommend that firms:

■ Delegate assignments, consistent with performance of high-quality work, to those who will provide the best value for the time spent.

■ Have the client approve the initial staffing and any staffing increases.

■ Not charge for educating junior personnel in basic substantive or procedural rules or law or principles.

■ Not charge learning time for replacing staff or professionals.

- Staff most routine hearings and meetings with a single professional.

- Conduct intra-office conferences and meetings only when necessary and appropriate.

- Not "double charge" for long distance travel time.

Guidelines quoted in "Billing Guidelines Drawn Up in Central District," *California Law Business*, 6 (Daily Journal Corporation, Feb. 10, 1992).

REQUIRED BY CLIENTS IN CASES OF FEE DISPUTES & ARBITRATIONS

One other arena in which time records can be reviewed is client disputes about legal services bills and the resulting arbitration for resolution. (Of course, the dispute may also be the subject of a lawsuit.) The arbitrator then will review the bills for their reasonableness, among other things. This is yet another reason all timekeepers must record and craft their time records carefully.

IMPORTANCE OF BILLING TIME ON CONTINGENCY CASES

Even though contingent fees are not based on the amount of time attorneys put in working on the case, there are situations in which a quantifiable amount of work is important in these cases. These most often arise when the attorney is dismissed or withdraws from the case before the conclusion. In some states, attorneys can still recover legal fees for worked performed—even though the attorney did not ultimately achieve the recovery—by showing the hours worked.

Of course, in addition to fee recovery, having detailed time records for certain types of cases still provides valuable law practice management information. For example, the firm may determine that the profit margin for handling sexual harassment cases—calculated from the value of the hours put into the cases subtracted from the contingent fees earned—means that the firm should concentrate on these cases.

IMPORTANCE OF BILLING TIME IN CORPORATE LAW DEPARTMENTS

Some in-house corporate law departments are now setting minimum billable hour requirements for their attorneys and legal assistants. At the very least, many corporations track the hours spent by their legal departments in performing legal services, even though no minimum goals have been set.

> The trend in tracking time and billing clients was inspired in part by the declining economy. When the legal department 'charges' its 'clients,' it allows them to see where their money is going. And with corporations more closely scrutinizing their bottom lines, many legal departments need to justify their existence. One way is to demonstrate with documentation how much more efficient and less expensive the department is compared to outside counsel.

Nance-Nash, "More In-Housers Billing Hours Now," *California Law Business*, 24 (Daily Journal Corporation, Jan. 27, 1992).

But the primary reason for keeping track of hours worked by in-house lawyers and legal assistants is that it provides important management information. Just as in law firms, keeping track of hours allows for case management, provides staffing information, and can be an important part of performance evaluations.

> "It's difficult to compare your internal costs to your external costs—and by that I mean outside counsel—unless you track hours," says Robert Berkow, national director for legal consulting at Ernst & Young.

> "For me, it's a very useful management tool," says Kent Riegel, general counsel at ICI Americas. It allows him . . . to track caseload and work loads for the 35 lawyers in the department. It also assists him in forecasting how much his in-house clients will use legal services, based on past use.

Varchaver, "Quantity Counts: The Push to Bill More Hours," *The American Lawyer*, 50 (Jan./Feb. 1992).

[T]ime sheets carry a message from the managing partners to the rest of the firm. The message defines the firm's conception of what law practice is all about: Law practice consists of generating chargeable time. The younger folks get the message, as they always do.

For them, the point is to spend time, or at least to record time. . . . In some firms they notice partners who simply contrive billable hours for themselves and for juniors working under them. These practices are winked at or shrugged at. . . . Accordingly, the younger lawyers learned how to contrive billable hours on their own.

Geoffrey C. Hazard, "Ethics," *The National Law Journal*, 19 (Feb. 17, 1992) (from a column appearing monthly).

3

The Ethics Of Time Billing

DON'T "PAD" YOUR TIME

"Padding" your time sheets means adding time that you did not work, expanding the time you did work, or billing clients for tasks for which they should not be charged. You should **never** let the pressure of meeting minimum billable hour requirements persuade you to pad your time sheets. Not only is this unethical in the sense of cheating the client, it is also wrong because it presents a false picture of your work to the firm's attorneys and managers. Falsifying time sheets begets a cynical approach to work in general:

[N]o group can get serious mental work out of its members at a rate [of] more than 2,000 [hours] per year across the board.

Worse, the practice is corrupting. Much of that billable time represents simply going through the motions. No small part of it is bogus. Worse still, lessons learned in manipulation of billable hours can be applied to other professional tasks. . . .

Geoffrey C. Hazard, "Ethics," *The National Law Journal*, 19 (Feb. 17, 1992) (from a column appearing monthly).

LEARN AND FOLLOW THE FIRM'S AND CLIENT'S POLICIES REGARDING BILLING

Most firms have policies for the preparation of hourly time sheets. If your firm also has specific guidelines on how to word time descriptions, what amounts of time to bill for phone calls, and whether partial time increments should be rounded up, for example, by all means follow them.

Unfortunately, sometimes firms' policies are not sufficiently detailed about what clients can be billed for in specific situations. For example, if you work on a matter for client A at the same time you are flying to a meeting on behalf of client B, should you bill both clients? Should client B be billed half the time required for travel? Is it considered permissible to bill for both travel **and** work time, even though this means that on a four-hour flight, client B is charged for four hours, and client A is charged two hours, for a total of six hours? If these questions are not addressed in your firm's policy statements, you will need to seek advice elsewhere. (*See* "Who to Ask About Firm's Billing Policies & Practices," below.)

In addition to firm policies about billing time, many corporate clients have developed specific guidelines for billing practices which they expect outside counsel to follow. One particular area of concern for clients is overstaffing:

We have made an effort to stop outside counsel from lawyering in a grand manner. We don't need two lawyers from the same firm representing us in the courtroom or at depositions, we don't always have to do extensive discovery.

Jan Charles Gray, Senior Vice President/General Counsel/Secretary, Ralphs Grocery Company (Los Angeles, California), quoted in Nance-Nash, "10 General Counsel Tell How They Control Fees,"

California Law Business, 18 (Daily Journal Corporation, Jan. 27, 1992).

It is your responsibility to make sure that you have a clear understanding of:

- what you can and **should** bill clients for,
- whether any restrictions on wording time descriptions exist, and
- what tasks or projects you should **not** bill to clients.

If you do not know—**before** you start working—what you should record as billable time, you may end up missing some appropriately billable time, recording time that cannot be billed, and running the risk that some of your time will be written off.

You should always check to see if the client for whom you are working has provided your firm with billing guidelines. If so, study them carefully. You can be sure you will be held to them.

We implemented extensive billing guidelines two years ago. It covers budgeting, expense control and staffing, and we expect outside counsel to adhere to each category. . . . We have a paralegal whose primary functions include monitoring bills, checking for deviations from the guidelines and intrinsic errors in [the bills].

Ibid., quoting Francis R. Tunney, Jr., Corporate Vice-President/General Counsel/Secretary, Allergan, Inc. (Irvine, California).

WHO TO ASK ABOUT FIRM'S BILLING POLICIES & PRACTICES

Whenever you have a question about billing that is not answered by either the firm's or client's written billing policies, the first person to ask is the attorney who gave you the assignment which prompted the question. Because this attorney is probably also billing time to this client, he or she should know if there are any special, albeit unwritten, requirements.

You may also ask any of the following people for guidance:

- the senior partner in your practice group,
- the manager for your department,

- the client's billing attorney, or
- your firm's administrator (or office manager), if appropriate.

Showing concern for correct billing practices will **always** be well received.

The larger the billing increment, the more the client is going to pay for all activities in the case, including minor ones. A five-minute phone call costs $50 when a $200-an-hour lawyer bills in quarter-hour increments, but only $20 when billed at tenths-of-an-hour. Clients need not accept a law firm's billing increments as standard and therefore non-negotiable.

Greenfield, "Five Early Warning Signs of Potential Overbilling," *Cutting Costs of Legal Services* (special supplement to *The Recorder*) (Oct. 1991).

4

General Policy Issues Affecting Time Billing

TIME BILLING INCREMENTS & ROUNDING UP

As outlined earlier (in **Chapter One**), each hour of billing time can be broken down into billing increments. Typically, billing hours are divided by quarter hours, every ten minutes, or even into six-minute packages:

■ In "quarter-hour" billing systems, timekeepers record .25, .5 or .75 increments of hours. This translates into fifteen, thirty and forty-five minutes, respectively.

- Under a "sixth of an hour" system, billing time is recorded in increments of .10, .20 and .40 of an hour. These numbers reflect ten, twenty and forty minutes.

- In a "tenth of an hour" system, timekeepers must track every six minutes of their time. The increments are recorded as .1, .5 or .8. These numbers translate to six minutes, a half hour, and 48 minutes.

Sometimes a variety of systems is used in the same firm. This may be because the firm has a policy to bill only six minutes for phone calls, but uses a quarter-hour system for billing all other legal services. Firms can also utilize different increments for different clients. Client A may require billings based on tenth-of-an-hour increments, while client B is billed on the firm's standard quarter-hour system. This allows the firm to meet the requirements of different clients.

Regardless of which system (or combination of systems) your firm uses, you must also determine whether the firm's policy favors "rounding up" time. For example, in a quarter-hour system, even if most phone calls don't last more than five minutes, the policy for a number of firms is to "round up" to the nearest quarter hour. Thus, a five-minute phone call will be billed at 15 minutes.

Other firms require timekeepers to "aggregate" their shorter time increments instead of rounding up. Under this system, a timekeeper would keep track of all five-minute phone calls with a client, but not bill these calls until they reached a total of 15 minutes. This way, the client will only be billed for the exact time used, fifteen minutes, instead of being billed fifteen minutes for **each** five-minute phone call. In this example, if the timekeeper's billing rate is $100 per hour, three five-minute phone calls would cost $75 if billed individually, but only $25 if the time was aggregated.

Phone calls and short letters are the most common tasks which present the rounding up or aggregating question. You will also find, however, that your work does not always conform itself to neat, precise increments. If you finish a project in an hour and 35 minutes, and your firm bills on the quarter-hour system, do you bill for an hour and 45 minutes? You would if your firm's policy was to round up time.

Some firms require rounding up only if the time worked is within five minutes of the official increment. For example, under a quarter-hour system, a 20-minute phone call would not be rounded up to 30 minutes, but a 25-minute phone call would be. With this approach, time is rounded up if it is close to the next increment, but "rounded down" if it is closer to the shorter time frame.

You can see that working under a "rounding up" policy would usually yield more billable time. This is why it is particularly important to understand your firm's policy on this issue—rounding up, rounding down, or even aggregating time—if it is not specifically written down.

HOW TO BILL FOR TIME SPENT TRAVELING

Most firms will have addressed this somewhat thorny issue specifically. Billing for time spent traveling, even if it's on a client's behalf, is a problem area because many clients know (or assume) that the timekeeper may also be working on other matters. Clients have also expressed real concerns about being billed full rates just for time spent traveling, especially when no substantive work is performed.

For example, a legal assistant is required to go from Los Angeles to New York to attend a document production. Having reviewed the request for production of documents before leaving the office, the efficient legal assistant takes work for another client to peruse while on the plane. Because the trip is required by client A's document production, client A will be billed for the flight time. However, because the legal assistant summarized depositions for client B while traveling, client B should also be charged for the time spent summarizing. What to do now? Do you bill for all your travel time as well as the time spent summarizing?

It depends on your firm's policy regarding billing while traveling. Some firms specify that travel time is to be billed at half the timekeeper's billing rate. Thus, if the flight takes four hours, and the timekeeper is ordinarily billed at $100 per hour, the client will be billed only $200, not $400, the full rate. This reduction is typically accomplished by using a special "Travel" code to charge the time.

Another method for reducing the charge for travel is to reduce the actual travel time by half. To follow the above example, the legal assistant would bill only two hours to client A instead of the four hours required for the flight. This accomplishes the same reduced rate for travel time, but client B would still be billed at full rates (and full time) for the deposition summaries. The legal assistant would then have six total hours to bill to clients (assuming the summaries occupied the entire flight time).

Some firms, however, require that travel time be billed at full rates, and that the entire time taken by traveling be charged. In these instances—as in the above example—the efficient timekeeper will be able to "expand time." By working on client B matters for four hours, during a four-hour flight for client A, the timekeeper can effectively bill for eight hours of work in a span of four hours. This practice is not at all unethical, but firms employing this policy for charging traveling time may find themselves forced to make a change by client demands.

Make sure you understand your firm's policy on travel time **before** embarking on a client business-related trip, even if it's just across town. If you do not bill for this time when you should, you will be shortchanging the firm, and you will have missed an opportunity to add to your billable hours total.

WORKING WITH SEVERE BILLING LIMITATIONS

In probate and bankruptcy cases, and in performing work for some insurance company clients, you will sometimes find that what you can bill the client for is severely restricted. (*See, e.g.*, the bankruptcy court requirements set forth earlier in **Chapter Two**, "Time Records Required by Courts in Fee Award Situations.") As with all client policies on billing, be sure you understand and follow these strictures. Even if this means that you must redraft your time descriptions to avoid problem areas, you should do so.

Remember that the billing attorney will ordinarily review the draft bills before they are sent to the client or filed with the court. If you have charged time that you should not have, or your time descriptions do not meet the requirements of the court or client, your time may be written off. You can often avoid this by simply rewording your time descriptions.

For example, if the client is sensitive about being billed for what it perceives are clerical tasks, do not describe your time spent putting numbers on documents as "put numbers on documents: 4 hours." Yes, that's a short description of what you did, but numbering documents is **not** simply a clerical task, and your time description should reflect this fact:

Assigned range of production numbers for documents produced by client; followed numbering scheme per guidelines to ensure documents contained in two bankers' boxes are ready for production: 4 hours.

One way to double check yourself is to ask if you would have objections if presented with a bill containing your time descriptions. (Refer to **Chapter Six** for further information on how to draft appropriate time descriptions.)

BILLING FOR ON-CALL TIME

Say the attorney you've been working with on a real estate deal asks you to be available on a weekend in case portions of the agreement need further research or rewriting. There's no way to know if your time will actually be needed, so while you don't have to go into the office, you also can't go out of town or be away from telephone access. Okay, the weekend is over, you didn't receive a frantic call to come into the office, but you did waste a perfectly beautiful weekend staying indoors by the phone when you could have gone skiing instead. Now what?

Do you bill the client for being available even if you didn't do any work? Do you bill administrative time to the firm? Do you just chalk it up to experience? It all depends on whether your firm's billing policies allow you to bill for this "on-call" time.

Some firms have agreements with particular clients that on-call time will be billed. This is reasonable, given that last-minute hitches in real estate or corporate deals can occur. But whether you can always bill for this kind of time depends on your firm's policies. If you find yourself in this situation, be sure to ask the assigning attorney **first** what to do about billing your time.

WHAT TASKS ARE CONSIDERED STRICTLY ADMINISTRATIVE TIME

Although this will also vary from firm to firm, some tasks are more often than not considered strictly administrative, and therefore, **not** chargeable to clients. Administrative time must still be accounted for even though it produces no revenue. How much time is being spent on administrative tasks can be an important piece of management information.

In some firms, administrative time is simply a shorthand reference for all nonbillable time. In others, this term carries a specific meaning. For the purposes of this monograph, "administrative time" refers to all nonbillable time. This includes time spent in the following areas. Frequently, firms will assign specific time billing codes to these separate categories of administrative time.

- vacation time off
- sick leave
- training time (you are being trained or you are training someone else)
- pro bono projects
- recruiting activities
- bar association activities
- continuing education (attendance at seminars, etc.)
- business promotion/client development/marketing
- lectures, teaching, writing projects
- office administration activities

It is very important that you use the correct code, even though this time will not be billed. For example, if you incorrectly allocate time to "writing projects" instead of "client development," this error will make the monthly and year-end management reports inaccurate. Sometimes certain administrative time categories are counted toward your billable hours requirement. If this is true for client development activities, to follow the above example, you may have effectively reduced the amount of time credited to your annual requirement.

The category of "office administration activities" generally encompasses firm business-oriented tasks, such as the following:

- completion of time sheets, reviewing billing records, conferences with billing attorneys
- organizing office files/records
- coordinating work with your secretary, when not specifically client work related
- attending meetings of firm committees (when another time category, such as recruiting, is inappropriate)
- general discussions with other firm members about non-client related matters
- reviewing advance sheets, legal newspapers, bar journals, etc.

You can also spend a great deal of time in other quasi-office administration tasks. Whether you can bill a client for this time will depend entirely on the circumstances:

- searching for a misplaced client file(s)
- searching for another member of the firm (for example, you need to ask an attorney a question in order to finish a client project)
- unjamming photocopy machines or other time delays due to equipment failures
- redoing a project that was originally client billable
- travel time between floors or offices to confer with colleagues
- waiting for colleagues to finish phone conversations (or other conferences) in anticipation of meeting about client-billable projects

It cannot be emphasized enough that in these circumstances, you need to consult your firm's billing policy, ask the billing attorney or confer with the attorney who has assigned you the particular project for guidance on whether this time can, or should, be billed to the client.

DETERMINING WHEN CLIENTS SHOULD BE CHARGED FOR OVERTIME

A number of law firms charge premium rates when overtime for secretaries, word processing staff or paralegals is necessary. The difficulty in applying this policy comes in deciding which client should be charged, when the delays causing the overtime were **not** the fault of the client for whom overtime was incurred.

For example, an attorney was unexpectedly busy all day in a deposition for client A. As a result, the project for client B that the attorney intended to meet with a paralegal about was delayed until after normal working hours. Because this meeting took place later than expected, and secretarial help was required, both the paralegal and the paralegal's secretary incurred overtime. Should the overtime be charged to client A or client B?

Typically, client B will be charged for the overtime, since it is on this client's behalf that the overtime was worked. But in this circumstance, you should ask whether overtime should be charged at all (or charged to client A), because it was the attorney's delay over a deposition for client A that caused the overtime. Check first with the attorney who assigned you the overtime project to see how the overtime charge should be handled.

You should also make sure that overtime has in fact been authorized. Even if the attorney requests that the project be completed the next day (to continue with the above example), he or she may not be aware that overtime is required to meet this deadline. The attorney also may not want you (or your secretary) to charge anyone for the overtime, since this is sometimes discretionary. **Always ask first.**

HOW TO BILL FOR TRIAL TIME

Sometimes, time spent preparing for and attending trial on behalf of a client is considered time subject to premium rates. If this is the situation in your firm, be aware that your time will be billed at a higher than normal rate, and therefore, the client might be scrutinizing the bill even more closely.

There is also substantial "down" time associated with trials. For example, you will wait for the judge to complete the morning docket call, there will usually be frequent recesses, and the lunch break can last anywhere from one to four hours. Such down time will usually not present problems, because you will find yourself fully occupied with getting prepared for the next witness, the next evidentiary wrangle, or the next battle with the judge. But if you do find yourself at loose ends while you're waiting for trial to recommence, do you bill this time?

Other billing questions will arise, particularly if you are a junior member of the trial team. Do you bill for time expended in getting lunch together for all members of the team? Do you bill for time spent finding an office supply store so you can buy more legal pads for the lead attorney? Do you bill for the time required to line up after-hours secretarial support? Always ask the attorney in charge.

HYPOTHETICAL BILLING SITUATIONS TO TEST YOUR SKILLS

Policies for billing time to clients vary widely between firms and corporate legal departments. You will also find that differences in billing practices exist between members of the same firm. One attorney may bill for time waiting to see a senior partner, while another may charge this as office administration time. *See* Prescott & Freidler, "Test Your Billing Skills on Five Hypotheticals," *California Law Business*, 20 (Daily Journal Corporation, Jan. 27 1992).

Described below are three hypothetical work situations which present difficult billing questions. You should apply what you know of your firm's billing guidelines, and the rules already detailed for you in this monograph to decide what tasks and amounts of time you should bill each client, or to administrative time categories.

Review your answers with your department manager, billing attorney or other person providing billing training or orientation, so you can see if—and how—you can improve your billing skills. Suggested answers to these hypothetical situations are provided at the end of this section.

Hypothetical Situation # 1. You have been assigned the project of reviewing two boxes of documents on behalf of Client A for possible claims of privilege. The documents must be reviewed, a log of potentially privileged documents created, and the documents must be numbered by the next day.

The first thing you do, after meeting for 45 minutes with the attorney who gave you the assignment, is to read up on what constitutes privilege. This task consumes two hours. You also talk with some colleagues for an hour about how they've conducted privilege reviews in the past.

Now, you're ready to start reviewing documents, but find you need some legal pads to record your notes. You go to the supply room on the floor above you, chat with the people working in that department, and come back down to your office. Obtaining the legal pads has consumed 30 minutes.

The actual review of documents takes three hours and ten minutes. Because you got started later in the day than you'd planned, you ask your secretary to stay overtime to type up the log you've created. You stay to proofread the log, make corrections and finalize the document, which takes a total of 20 minutes. While you wait for the document to be typed, you scan the latest issue of *The American Lawyer* for 20 minutes. Proofreading, correcting and finalizing has taken 30 minutes, while your reading time equalled 50 minutes. Your secretary has worked one hour and 20 minutes on overtime.

Now that the project is finished, you take 25 minutes to put away the boxes and make copies of the privilege document log. You spend the next ten minutes generally straightening up your office.

How do you bill your time if you work in a firm that utilizes the quarter-hour system? The sixth-of-an-hour system? Assume that your firm has adopted a "rounding up" policy.

Hypothetical Situation # 2. You've been asked to work on the firm's computer committee, have just brought on a new real estate client, Client B, and have a recruiting dinner to attend. Here's how your day goes.

In the morning, you call client B just to touch base on whether their office has received the retainer agreement your secretary sent over last week. You chat about baseball and the upcoming World Series for ten minutes, and then get down to business. The client has some concerns about the retainer agreement, which you address satisfactorily in about ten minutes. You close the conversation with a promise to get together soon for lunch, and spend about three minutes checking your calendar and making a date.

While you were on the phone, your secretary places two letters for your signature, one to Client C and one to Client D, in front of you. You quickly scan and sign them while you continue talking.

After the conversation ends, you go down the hall to chat with the head of the real estate section to assure him that Client B is on board. This conversation takes about 35 minutes, but you also discuss other matters.

You're now due for a meeting of the computer committee which you expect will be a long one. So, you tell your secretary to interrupt you if necessary, which he does, several times. None of the interruptions is significant except for one, which requires you to take a lengthy call from Client D. You're on the phone for 20 minutes.

Finally, the committee meeting—which lasted three hours total, although a half hour was used just for lunch—is over and you can get down to work. You review real estate documents for Client D for two hours, but you're interrupted several times by a junior attorney who is handling a matter for Client C. These interruptions together total about 30 minutes.

You take about 20 minutes to record your time and chat with your secretary about tomorrow's work schedule. You and two other real estate attorneys go out to dinner with an experienced legal assistant the firm is trying to recruit. Dinner lasts two hours.

How do you bill your time if you work in a firm that utilizes the quarter-hour system?

Hypothetical Situation # 3. You need to travel across town to meet with Client E on a litigation matter, for which you just spent an hour and a half preparing. The trip normally takes 45 minutes, but today, for some reason, the freeways are jammed and it takes an hour and 25 minutes. You finally arrive, only to find that the person you were supposed to be meeting with had to take a conference call.

As a result, you cool your heels in the reception area for 15 minutes. The meeting about the litigation finally starts, and takes three hours. You get back on the freeway to go back to the office, and this time the trip runs more smoothly, taking the expected 45 minutes.

When you arrive back at your office, you discover several messages from the senior partner on the litigation matter for Client E. You go to her office, but she's on the phone. Even though you signal that you can come back later, the partner waves at you to come on in and wait. That conversation lasts 15 minutes while you wait, leafing through an old issue of *Trial* magazine.

You tell the partner about your meeting at the client's offices that morning, elaborating in great detail about the delay caused by the freeway jam up. The discussion of the client matter consumes about 30 minutes, but you spend a total of 45 minutes talking with the partner about other matters too. Because the partner wants to touch base with Client E to see how things stand, she calls the person you met with that morning while you're still in the office. Although the call is conducted on the speaker phone, the partner doesn't mention your presence. This call lasts ten minutes.

When you finally get back to your office, your secretary is getting ready to go home. You ask her to stay for just another 30 minutes, even though this means she'll be on overtime, so you can get your notes of the morning's meeting typed up. The notes aren't really needed for the next day, but you like to have notes of meetings memorialized as soon as possible. While your secretary is typing up your notes, you spend 30 minutes trying to figure out how to bill your time for the day.

How do you bill your travel and waiting time? And what should you do about the secretarial overtime?

Suggested Answers to Hypotheticals. In *Hypothetical # 1*, the total time worked is either 9.25 hours under the quarter-hour system, or 9.0 hours under the sixth-of-an-hour system. Client billable time under either system is either seven hours or five hours, depending upon whether the two hours spent boning up on what constitutes privilege is considered general training time or chargeable to the client. Likewise, the time allocated to training would be either one or three hours, depending upon how your firm would answer this question.

You can see the differences between the two increment systems in the administrative time, because rounding up in quarter-hour increments results in 1.25 hours, but under the other system, only

1.0 hour was accumulated. The secretarial overtime is reasonably charged to the client, even though it was necessitated in part because of your own work schedule, not client demands.

Because *Hypothetical # 2* is much more complicated, each opportunity to bill will be addressed in turn. The baseball discussion and checking your calendar for lunch could either be charged to client development or not billed at all. However, the discussion about the retainer should definitely be billed to client development. Signing letters while you were on the phone could either be charged at the lowest increment for Clients C and D or not billed at all. At least part of the conversation with the head of the real estate section should be charged to client development, but it depends on whether this was the primary point of the conversation.

The computer committee meeting is an easier call. Even though the meeting lasted a total of three hours, a half hour was spent just on lunch. You should only bill 2.0 hours to firm committee activities, because you also took a call from Client D during this meeting. This 20-minute call should be billed to the client at either .5 or .15, depending on whether your firm rounds up or down.

The next client billable time is for Client D, but because you were interrupted with questions about Client C, bill 1.5 hours to D and .5 to C. Finally, at the end of the day, you have either .5 or .15 hours of administrative time, again, depending on the rounding up/down policy. The two-hour dinner should be charged to firm recruiting activities.

Hypothetical # 3 presents the troublesome travel question. Remember that ordinarily, travel time is billed to clients. Firms take different stances on this issue, however, sometimes billing at reduced rates or for only half the time spent traveling. It may even be that you should charge only the **normal** travel time, not for the additional time caused by the traffic jam. Therefore, in this hypothetical, you will probably treat your travel time differently from straight client billable time.

Most of your time is client billable, but the time spent waiting while the client was on a conference call could either be billed or accounted for as administrative time. The fact that you had to wait was neither your nor the client's fault.

Now, what to do about the time you spent waiting for the partner? Your purpose for being there is to tell her about the client meeting, but this does not mean that your waiting time is client billable. A similar problem arises for the time you spend listening to the call between the partner and the client. Because you took no part in the conversation—**nor** was the client told you were present—chances are you should not bill your time. If your presence had been announced, the client would expect to see a charge for this time. What you should have done is ask the partner as soon as the conversation ended whether you should bill your time.

You should **not** charge the client for your secretary's overtime to type up your meeting notes. This was not required for the client, it was a matter of file housekeeping only. And, finally, your time spent trying to figure all this out so you could complete your time sheets is office administrative time only, of course.

Remember, the above answers are only suggested. You should check your firm's billing guidelines and specific client policies, if any, to determine the correct answers for your own firm.

The source of information for invoices is your time records. If you recorded everything you did, then preparing the invoice will simply be a matter of transferring the services rendered from your time records to the invoices.

J. Foonberg, *How to Start and Build a Law Practice*, 205 (American Bar Association 1976).

5

The Mechanics of Timekeeping

BILL ALL YOUR TIME—DON'T EDIT YOURSELF

Unless you know for sure that certain tasks are not billable to clients or should legitimately be allocated to an administrative category, you should bill all your time to the appropriate client. In this context, "billing time" means accounting for **all** the time you either spend working on client projects or on firm-related business. Of course, firm-related business includes client development, bar association activities, continuing legal education, recruiting, etc.

If you have a question about whether time should be billed to a client, by all means ask the appropriate person for guidance. But don't **preclude** billing that time at all just because you're unsure. The same rule applies to administrative, or firm-related tasks. It's important to account for all your working time, because if you don't:

- the management reports that are so important for decision making will be incorrect

- the picture of your individual working record, captured in both monthly and annual reports, will be incorrect

- if you fail to bill clients for time that should have been billed, you're costing the firm revenue

Remember, it's much better to ask billing questions to get it right the first time. These questions will be well received, and before long, you'll have a better understanding of the firm's and clients' policies.

WRITE DOWN YOUR TIME EVERY DAY, NOT ONCE A MONTH

Yes, I'm sure you've heard of attorneys who wait until the end of the month (or even longer), to write up their time sheets. Some timekeepers have been known to simply estimate their time spent on client matters. They tell their secretaries: "Just ball park it."

Don't do this.

Really, DON'T do this.

Believe me, you will live to regret it if you do. Once, I supervised a legal assistant who was very involved in preparing for a trial, and the last thing he wanted to do every day was fill out time sheets. So, he didn't. For two months.

First, he thought he'd be able to catch up real quickly. Sure, no problem, he told me: "I'll just go through my calendar and reconstruct those days."

Well, not only was he working on trial preparation during these two months, he'd handled several other matters as well. And without detailed notes regarding his activities, he could only reconstruct about three-fourths of the time I knew he'd spent. This meant that the firm was denied several hours of client billable time, and thus revenue, not only because he couldn't remember all of the time, but because the time he could remember was so late being billed, that some clients naturally objected. And if this wasn't bad enough by itself, the agony of trying to reconstruct all those days and hours was **awful.**

You have a responsibility to the firm you work for to record **all** your time. This is especially true of client-billable time. To do this efficiently, effectively and ethically, **you must contemporaneously record information about your time.** If you get into the habit of writing down your time billing information every day—**religiously**—you will be rewarded by:

- earning more money for your firm
- never having to reconstruct days (or weeks) of time, and
- ensuring that your own time record reports are accurate.

REVIEW OF VARIOUS TIME SHEET FORMS & VALUE OF DIRECT INPUT TO COMPUTER SYSTEMS

The basic information needed to bill your time is:

- your **name or initials**; sometimes firms even assign specific identification codes to timekeepers particularly in large firms, where initials can be repeated (say there are several "NJMs" in the firm);

- the **client identification code,** usually a combination of alpha characters (sometimes the first three letters of the client name), and a series of numbers, such as "ABC-123," which would stand for Atlas Book Company, matter number 123;

- the appropriate **client matter number,** used for clients who have several matters with the firm; for example, if the firm is handling five litigation cases, two real estate deals and one corporate offering for Atlas Book Company;

- the **total time** spent on a particular task in the appropriate time increments, and rounded up (if that is firm policy), to the nearest increment;

- the **date the work was performed;** and

■ **a description of the work performed,** for example: "Researched title records for XYZ Development; annotated research file for responses to EPA documents."

Providing the above information is essential to proper time billing. Filling out your firm's time sheets correctly—the first time around—will help ensure **prompt** billing of clients.

On most time sheets, the timekeeper fills out special boxes for certain pieces of information. This is especially true for client/matter number and date information. You will most likely be given some filled-in time sheets to use as examples. If not, ask your supervising attorney or secretary (if this person will be handling your time sheet input), for guidance on filling out these forms.

Sometimes the description field is also limited in the number of characters that can be used. In these cases, firms devise **shorthand references and abbreviations** for verbs and standard tasks, such as the following:

■ ap: appearance at
■ az: analyze
■ ca: court appearance
■ dp: deposition
■ fi: filing
■ lt: letter
■ op: opposing counsel
■ oc: office conference
■ rv: review
■ rr: review and revise
■ tc: telephone conversation
■ wc: with client

Each firm has its own shorthand references. Most often you'll be given a list of these references to use when you're instructed how to fill out the time sheets. If not, ask the billing department or your secretary about the shorthand annotations which are employed in your firm.

There are almost as many different forms of time sheets as they are policies for billing time. Some firms have designed their own forms, while others use commercially printed forms that are avail-

able through legal stationery companies. A sample time sheet form
follows.

SAMPLE HOURLY BILLING TIME SHEET

TIMEKEEPER NAME/INITIALS   **MJW**   DATE   **5/28/92**

Client   **ATLAS BOOK CO.**   Matter # **202**   Time   **4.75**

Time Description: **Prepare for deposition of expert witness Jones in Prescott matter; review file for pertinent information; instruct legal assistant on preparation of witness notebook**

Client   **KLM, INC.**   Matter # **519**   Time   **1.25**

Time Description: **Telecons w/client representative Johnson; draft notes re appeal strategy for the Evans appeal file**

Client   **SCHMIDT, ALLEN**   Matter # **001**   Time   **2.5**

Time Description: **Initial case meeting with client; review facts of employment discrimination allegations by engineer applicants; draft notes to file**

Client   **FIRM/Committee**   Matter # **997**   Time   **1.0**

Time Description: **Attend associate committee meeting**

Client   **FIRM/Administration** Matter # **990**   Time   **.75**

Time Description: **Time billing; file organization; to-do list**

Total Time   **10.25**   Billable **8.5**   Nonbillable   **1.75**

Time sheets are generally printed showing several segments for billing different clients. For example, some forms have five separate segments, like the earlier example. This form allows a timekeeper to bill five clients, or five different matters for the same client. Sometimes a single time sheet will not be sufficient to allocate all your time for one day. This is especially true if your work is very fragmented, that is, you work on a number of different projects for short periods of time in a single day. In these situations, you might have to use several time sheets for one day's work.

Some time sheets employ a perforated top sheet with a self carbon back page. This form allows the timekeeper to record the time into the segments, and also have a carbon of the day's efforts. Then, once the time sheet has been completely filled out, the perforated segments are torn into **"time slips."** These slips can then be separated by client number. This facilitates computer entry of the time slips completed for the same client, because they can be collated by client number. The self-carbon sheet also provides timekeepers with a daily time record.

This "time slip" approach is accomplished also by "peel off" segments. With these types of forms, the top sheet is divided into different client segments, and has a self adhesive on the back side. Once the time sheet is filled out, the different segments can be lifted off the backing sheet and affixed to separate client/matter pages.

Regardless of the particular form of time sheet used, there is a **better, more efficient way** to record your billable and nonbillable time. If your firm has computer terminals available, it may be possible to **key in your time records directly** into the firm's client billing database. This would mean that the only "time sheet" you have to fill out is the one on the computer screen.

It's very efficient to key in your own time, and not only because this obviates the need for a second person to handle the input. It also means that you can double check your data entry as you go. You won't need to wait for a print out of your secretary's work to make sure the entry of your time records is correct. Also, if you can enter your time as you work during the day—just as you would do if you were filling out a hard copy time sheet—you will most likely capture more of your billable time.

USING "DIARY" TO KEEP TRACK OF TIME WORKED

You will find that using a "diary" form of daily calendar is a great way to keep up with all the time you work. These types of calendars have one or two pages for each day. The days are divided into time segments, usually in fifteen-minute spans.

A common diary starts charting the time of day at 7:00 a.m., and provides spaces to write information for each fifteen minutes until 7:00 p.m. Others use different starting and ending times. Still other time diaries allow you to fill in the appropriate times yourself, while providing a chart of hours broken into 15-minute segments. Your firm's office supply department (or person) can usually find a diary system that will fit your hours and needs.

Using a diary type of calendar allows you to keep track of your entire day, as illustrated by the following example.

SAMPLE WORK DIARY

■ 9:00 a.m. to 10:30 a.m.

ABC-123 / Review complaint; take notes on possible answer issues [1.5 hours]

■ 10:30 a.m. to 11:15 a.m.

TOC-456 / Conference with RJN re trial preparation status; set meeting with client [.75 hour]

■ 11:15 a.m. to 12:30 p.m.

FIR-678 / Meeting with TJS re trial brief in Jones matter; begin research on RICO issues [1.25 hours]

■ 12:30 p.m. to 1:30 p.m.

Lunch [1 hour]

■ 1:30 p.m. to 4:15 p.m.

FIR-678 / Resume research on requirements to file complaint based on RICO violations; take notes of possible complaint language; conference with law librarian re newspaper articles on proof of multiple RICO violations [2.75 hours]

■ 4:15 p.m. to 4:30 p.m.

Admin / Conference with secretary [.25 hour]

■ 4:30 p.m. to 5:15 p.m.

TOC-901 / Telephone conference with client re status of case; draft file memorandum [.75 hour]

■ 5:15 p.m. to 7:45 p.m.

FIR-678 / Finish research on RICO issues; conference with TJS re results of research; begin drafting complaint language [2.5 hours]

■ 7:45 p.m. to 8:00 p.m.

Admin / Time sheets [.25 hour]

Now, you can go back through your diary each day and fill out time sheets easily. You show the time spans worked, so you can easily calculate the total time to be billed for each client/matter. You've noted the client and matter numbers, and also written fairly comprehensive descriptions of the work performed. And, since this record is kept on the appropriate date page of your calendar, you have all the information you need ready at hand. In the above example, client billable time is 9.5 hours; nonbillable, administrative time is .5 hour.

DAILY OR WEEKLY CALENDAR NOTES

If you keep close track of your workload on your daily or weekly desk calendar, you can also use these notes to create your time sheets. In this case, you would note all appointments, meetings and deadline events. You might also use your desk calendar to make notes of scheduled telephone calls, due dates for projects and target dates for status reports or for completing projects. While a daily calendar usually provides sufficient space to also note a brief description of the work performed, you may find the writing space on monthly desk calendars too limited.

Sometimes, the best approach is to keep both a diary of time worked and a desk calendar. Your desk calendar can be used to keep track of appointments, due dates and upcoming events. Then when you're completing your time sheets by transferring information from the diary, you can double check the desk calendar to see if you failed to note any time. You may find that although you've noted a meeting or appointment on your calendar that did in fact occur, but you simply failed to separate out that time in the diary. This way, you have a double check on your records.

REVIEWING CHRONOLOGICAL FILES TO RECONSTRUCT TIME

Another good way to double check whether you've captured all your billable time is to review your chronological file. Chronological files (also called "chron" files), are simply files containing all the documents you author and/or receive on a daily basis, kept in date order. Thus, if you think you may have missed some time, you can review this file and perhaps find two or three short letters you wrote to a client which you failed to note in your diary or on your calendar.

Some people who conduct extensive correspondence find it sufficient to rely almost solely on their chronological files to reconstruct their billable time. This is NOT recommended. In the first place, not every piece of billable time is associated with correspondence. Even if your chron files are very representative of your work day, you will not always know—from the context of the correspondence—who should be billed for the time. And, of course, there is no record of how much time was spent in drafting and finalizing the correspondence. But, by all means, use your chronological files as a double check on your records.

HAVING YOUR SECRETARY KEEP RECORDS OF CALLS, CONFERENCES & MEETINGS

Your secretary can be another great source of information about your work day. Depending on whether your secretary screens your calls and takes messages in your absence (as opposed to having voice mail), you can frequently review the records of these calls to prompt your memory. Often, phone calls are the shortest, and therefore most easily forgotten, uses of your time. Ask your secretary to note who calls you throughout the day. Then, you can review this list and make sure you've billed the time used.

Even if your firm does employ a voice mail system, if you have the option of saving your messages throughout the day, do so. In most systems, you can then scan the messages quickly. You'll occasionally find phone calls that you failed to note for the time sheets.

Your secretary can also be of great assistance in keeping track of who goes into your office, particularly those people who stay for a while. Of course, not all visiting people will have something to do with billable activities, but most will. And, by noting all your visitors throughout the day, your secretary can provide you with another very helpful double-check list.

To coordinate your workload with your secretary, you should keep him or her informed of your work plans. At some point each week, review your schedule for the next week with your secretary. Mention all anticipated appointments, conference calls and meetings. Sometimes, it's also a good idea to do this on a daily basis.

Not only will your secretary have a better idea about what work to expect, he or she will also have an thorough overview of your workload. Of course, you should also keep your secretary informed of your whereabouts every time you leave the office. When your secretary knows what you are doing and what you have planned, he or she can help immensely with your timekeeping responsibilities.

Partners [and all timekeepers] should put themselves in the shoes of the general counsel who has to take a legal bill to his or her CEO and explain or justify the bottom-line cost. Drafting bills that are truly descriptive of what is accomplished and where the price accurately reflects the useful time spent by the firm's lawyers [and legal assistants], will be greatly appreciated.

Prescott & Freidler, "Test Your Billing Skills on Five Hypotheticals," *California Law Business*, 21 (Daily Journal Corporation, Jan. 27 1992).

6

Ensuring Time Billed Is Actually Charged to the Client

HURDLES TO OVERCOME IN BILLING TIME

There are always at least three hurdles to overcome in billing time. Not doing your part to meet any one of these will result in reduced billable hours, and therefore reduced revenue for your firm.

■ capturing all your appropriately billable time;

■ presenting time records to the billing attorney that will be perceived as time well spent, and therefore not written off or written down; and

■ convincing the client—by drafting appropriate descriptions of the work performed—that this was indeed time well spent, so the bill will be paid without reduction.

If you can deal effectively with the above challenges, you will have met your responsibilities as a timekeeper. And, now that you have learned the first step—how to capture all your time—you're ready to meet the next two hurdles.

IMPORTANCE OF WORKING WITHIN TIME BUDGET FOR ASSIGNMENTS

A "time budget" is the total amount of time that the attorney giving you an assignment expects you to spend on the project. For instance, the attorney tells you that you should spend only ten hours on a research project. If your work takes longer than ten hours, and you bill for this time **without** obtaining the attorney's okay, you may find that the total will be reduced by the billing attorney.

Time budgets should **not** be confused with deadlines for completion of projects. The deadline for turning in your results may be the middle of next week, but the attorney may only expect you to spend just a few hours on the task assigned. You should **always** ask the attorney for a time budget, if he or she doesn't give you one. If you do request or budget,

■ the attorney will not be surprised by the time you spend, because you've already discussed it; and
■ you can make sure that your expectations for the scope of the project matches the attorney's.

For example, the attorney may be under the impression that this project should take about four hours, but from past experience, you know that it will most likely take two days. This lack of agreement could result from the attorney not understanding everything that is involved to accomplish the project. But it may also be that you don't understand the limited scope of the work that the attorney has in mind. It's also possible that the client is on a strict budget, and the attorney is trying to keep the bill down.

If you address the time budget issue up front, you can prevent any later misunderstandings. But more importantly, you will also avoid later write-offs of time that may perceived by the billing attorney as excessive for the task, or not authorized. This way, you can help make sure that all the time you bill actually does get charged to the client.

PROVIDE REGULAR STATUS REPORTS TO ASSIGNING ATTORNEY

It is your responsibility to provide status reports to the attorneys who assign you projects. And, don't expect them to ask you for updates: busy attorneys usually don't have the time. Keeping the attorneys for whom you are working informed about your progress is very important, both for your personal success on the job, and for getting past the billing attorney "hurdle."

If the billing attorney has questions regarding time that you have billed, often he or she will question the attorney in charge about the amount of time. If you've kept your supervising attorney informed of your progress (or lack thereof), then he or she will have a ready answer. But if the attorney cannot provide a justification for your time, chances are it will be written down or even written off.

Your status reports should include the following information:

- hours billed to date
- percentage of time budget used
- anticipated additional time required (if any), and
- expected completion date

Of course, on short-turnaround projects, your status reports will consist of simple and brief conversations. But on longer-term projects—especially those spanning weeks or months—and assignments which are ongoing, you should provide **written status reports.**

Make your status reports easy to follow and quick to read. A good rule of thumb for the right amount of detail to include is what's called a "15/5" memorandum. This memorandum takes no more than fifteen minutes to write and only five minutes to read. That's all you really need to do, and you can address the above issues easily in this amount of time.

SAMPLE STATUS REPORT

TO: Michael J. Williams

FROM: Sam F. Benjamin

DATE: March 9, 1992

RE: Status Report on Johnson Brothers, Inc. v. O'Keefe Co.

        Scope of Project: Review 20 boxes of client records for responsiveness to Defendant's First Request for Production

        Date assigned: 3/2/92

        Date due: 3/16/92

        Time allotted: 60 to 75 hours

Status: I have indexed the files contained in all 20 boxes of documents. That index was finalized 3/4/92 and given to your secretary. This aspect of the project required 8 hours.

I have also reviewed 12 of the boxes, and have flagged approximately 425 pages of documents as being responsive to the discovery request. **Some of these documents may also be privileged, however, due to attorney advice that is mentioned. Thus, these documents will also require your review.**

This portion of the review has taken 32 hours, for a total of 40 hours billed to Johnson Brothers, Inc. to date.

I anticipate finishing the project by 3/13/92, and I expect the balance of the document review will require 25 more hours. The total time required will **not** exceed the time budget provided.

WHEN PROJECTS REQUIRE MORE TIME THAN BUDGETED OR EXPECTED

Let the attorney know—as soon as possible—when you determine that the project you're working on will take more time than expected or budgeted. If you just keep working on your own, and billing more time to the project, you run the risk of having all the time worked over the budget limitation written off. Remember, time budgets exist for a reason: the attorney most likely knows what the task is worth to the client and how much time should be expended.

There are many reasons that you may not be able to meet the time budget for a particular project. For example:

- you may be doing more than is required,
- the project is more complicated than either you or the attorney anticipated,
- you may have misunderstood the scope of the original assignment,
- one of your other assignments was suddenly given a higher priority, or
- you may not be managing your time as effectively as you would like.

Regardless of the reasons, if you exceed the time budget limitation—**without** getting the attorney's okay to expend more time—you've not given yourself a chance to explain these problems to the attorney. If the attorney knows you need more time, chances are it will be authorized. Once you receive authorization, you will have done your part to ensure that this time will not be written off.

WRITING TIME DESCRIPTIONS TO ENSURE PERCEPTIONS THAT YOUR TIME WAS WELL SPENT

Remember the discussion of hourly time billing as the "product" that a law firm "sells"? Client invoices are somewhat akin to the "packages" for that legal services product. If this package describes the product's "contents" well, and the contents are perceived as something the client needs—and therefore values—then the bill will most likely be paid, if not happily, at least promptly.

Your time billing efforts will play a large part in making the package attractive to the client. This is accomplished by crafting detailed time descriptions. At a minimum, the information you provide about the work you performed should:

- be specific about the work described, not generic
- describe with particularity the steps involved in the work you performed
- mention the specific documents you reviewed
- mention all the documents you drafted, and specify whether it was the first or second draft, etc.
- describe the course of research, mentioning some of the materials researched
- show every single date you worked on a matter, even if only a minor service was rendered
- document all phone calls and conversations
- for work on pending lawsuits, always show the name of the case, court where the matter is pending, and perhaps the case number, if this information will not be clear from the client and matter number alone
- likewise, for corporate and real estate matters, list the name of the property or stock offering involved, or other specific identifying information

In a chapter titled "How to Word Invoices that Clients Are Happy to Pay," author Jay G. Foonberg gives the following advice: "The basic secret to invoicing is to tell the client everything you did. There is no such thing as an invoice that is too long." Foonberg, *How to Start and Build a Law Practice*, 208 (American Bar Association, 1976). If you follow this advice, you shouldn't go wrong.

What follows are several examples of poor time descriptions, along with suggested replacements:

- 1.75   "Pull documents from boxes."

   A better description is: "Conference with EJW; locate all documents required for EJW's review in preparation for upcoming motion for summary judgment in Jones v. Smith."

■ 3.75   "Prepare notice of appeal."
A better description is: "Conference w/NJT re preparation of appeal for Williams v. Essex Co.; review similar appeal filed in Taft v. Essex Co.; prepare first draft of notice for NJT review."

■ 5.25   "Organize documents for use as exhibits."
A better description is: "Review, index and organize into chronological order, three boxes of documents for use as exhibits in Johnson v. Johnson trial for ASJ."

■ 1.5   "Review title report for TJY Realty."
A better description is: "Retrieve and review title report prepared for CT Title Company on behalf of TJY Realty's possible acquisition of 1400 5th Avenue lot and building."

■ 8.5   "Prepare for Jones trial."
A better description is: "Review trial notebooks prepared for Jones v. Jackson trial; research and draft motion in limine; prepare outline of direct examination; draft opening statement for jury; research voir dire restrictions; conferences with TK and PLW re further finalization of trial exhibits."

■ 3.75   "Research Blue Sky filing requirements for offering."
A better description is: "Conference w/RTJ re requirements for initial stock offering for Ajax Co.; research Blue Sky filing requirements; draft memorandum re results of initial research for RTJ review."

■ 4.25   "Attend meeting with General Counsel re work on Smith matter."
A better description is: "Prepare for meeting re progress of Smith v. ABC Co.—review pleading and correspondence files; attend meeting with ABC Co. General Counsel, R. Johnston, re progress of firm handling of Smith lawsuit; review options for proceeding with appeal."

■ 2.75   "Number documents."
A better description is: "Assign range of production numbers for document production scheduled for Masterson
v. Essex Co. in response to Request for Documents dated
5/9/92; affix appropriate production numbers to documents contained in five boxes."

■ .5   "Telephone conference with client."
A better description is: "Telephone conference with Janet
Smithson, General Counsel, regarding copyright questions involved in acquisition of Rockola Music Co.; draft
note of conversation for acquisition file."

What all the suggested replacement descriptions have in common is they:

■ provide the additional detail and information required to
clearly identify the matter involved,

■ explain **why the work performed was necessary,** and

■ list **who else was involved** in the particular project.

Note also that the better descriptions mention all preparatory work
such as conferences, and follow-up work, such as drafting notes to
the file.

Including these types of details helps educate clients about why
the time billed might be more than they had expected. It also aids
the perception that this was time well spent. When drafting time
descriptions, always keep in mind how they will be viewed by the
client, and ask yourself whether you'd be happy paying a bill
containing the descriptions you've just written.

SAMPLE CLIENT BILL

Jones, Fahey & Greenberg, P.C.

To: Sharon R. Russell, General Counsel **Date:** May 18, 1992
Atlas Book Co.
123 W. 5th Street
Oklahoma City, OK 77098

Fees & Expenses for Legal Services—April 1992: $1,104.50

Jones v. Atlas Book Co.

| **Rose L. Miller:** | **5.25 hours @ $125/hr** | **$656.25** |

4/15/92: Conference with EJW; review all pleadings and produced discovery documents relating to preparation for upcoming motion for summary judgment in Jones matter; begin drafting motion.

| **Robert J. Wallis:** | **3.75 hours @ $80/hr** | **$300.00** |

4/13/92: Assign range of production numbers for document production scheduled for Jones matter in response to Request for Documents dated 4/9/92; affix appropriate production numbers to documents contained in five boxes.

Expense Items:		**$148.25**
Photocopies:	322 copies @ .20/each	$65.00
Messenger Charges:	3 trips @ $20/each	$60.00
Telephone Charges:	5 long distance calls	$23.25

Time management skills are more important than ever. The ability to determine priorities quickly and meet all deadlines is a skill that anyone can develop. But lawyers [and legal assistants] who don't take responsibility for themselves in these two areas are operating at a significant disadvantage when being considered for [advancement]. One of the most simple, yet often overlooked tools, is the maintenance of a single sheet of paper listing all active client matters that the lawyer [or legal assistant] is handling. A quick review of this list each morning can go a long way toward keeping [you] ahead of the workload.

Friedler & Prescott, "Associates Still Have Control of Their Destiny," *California Law Business*, 23 (Daily Journal Corporation, Feb. 24, 1992).

7

Time Management Tools

USE "TO DO" LISTS TO IDENTIFY PRIORITIES

Keeping your work prioritized is critical in a law practice. You may have ten (or more) different projects that you're working on at any given time. In order to complete them all on schedule, and to give each one the time required, you need to approach your work in a systematic and organized fashion.

"To do" lists are a great way to accomplish this goal. Start each week with a list of the major projects that must be accomplished that week. List them in order of priority, and then list the component steps for accomplishing the project. Check each step off as it is completed. Not only will this help keep your work focused, it also provides another double check for time keeping purposes.

SAMPLE TO-DO LIST

Week of June 15, 1992

Atlas Book Co.—Jones matter

Finalize, proofread and cite check trial brief

- ✓ review first draft for final corrections
- ✓ double check that corrections have been made
- ✓ line up JPT to handle cite checking

Double check on expert witness status

- ✓ conference with JPT
- ✓ confirm subpoenas served by XT service company

Confirm staffing for copying, exhibit tabbing and collation of exhibit notebooks

- ✓ check with JPT on status

Schmidt—Employment discrimination matter

Conference call with Schmidt's paralegal

- ✓ review file before call

Review applicant flow records from client

- ✓ check with JPT on organization of records into chronological order

Firm—Client Development

Lunch meeting with General Counsel of Essex Co.

- ✓ review Administrator's research re stock prices, planned changes in company

Firm—Committee

Finalize report for Paralegal Committee on billing rates

- ✓ check with secretary re collection of survey data
- ✓ talk with RY re recommendation
- ✓ ask Accounting Dept. to prepare spreadsheet re impact of changes in billing rates

Some people prefer to prepare lists of projects to do each day. However, if you focus solely on each day's tasks, you can sometimes lose track of the bigger picture. You may also become discouraged if you find that you cannot, in fact, complete the items on your daily to-do lists. You don't always have that much control over how your day's work will proceed. You may be called in for a last-minute conference. Or a project that had been a lower priority suddenly gets very hot. Then, all at once, your plan for that day's work is shot.

Making a list of the projects that you should reasonably be able to accomplish in one week avoids these problems. Also, looking at an entire week provides you an opportunity to review work loads with your secretary, to plan timing of work on multiple projects and evaluate competing projects and priorities. Always consider where you can put your time so that it will do the most good:

> Acquire the habit of evaluating tasks in terms of payoff. Think of time as a return on investment. You wouldn't spend three hours to find a $5 bargain and then devote ten minutes to a $5,000 investment decision. Why, then, devote an hour to a task that affords little or no payoff in terms of your goals and responsibilities, meanwhile losing time from a project that might lead to a major business coup?

S. Winston, *The Organized Executive*, 129 (Warner Books, 1983).

SET ASIDE CERTAIN TIMES TO PERFORM REGULAR TASKS

Just as you should take the time every day to prepare your time sheets (or input time directly into the computer), you should also set aside particular times to handle other regular tasks. That way, you will have already set aside time, you will get in the habit of performing the tasks, and you will have more structure to your working week or day.

Daily tasks should be grouped together as much as possible and scheduled for the same time every day. For instance, you could review your mail and meet with your secretary in the morning when you first arrive. You could also write up your time sheets from the day before as a way of reviewing the tasks accomplished. Then, you're ready to begin a new day.

The same is true for regular weekly tasks, such as conferring with your secretary about the next week's events. You may also want to schedule a weekly time to review last week's time sheet entries, check your chronological file for possibly missing time, and to generally reorganize your office for the upcoming week's activities. Many people in law firms also set aside time each week to catch up on reading advance sheets, legal periodicals and newspapers.

It really doesn't matter what time of day or at what point during the week you schedule these daily and weekly tasks. That's much more a matter of personal preference and working style. The point is to set aside regular time periods to handle these chores, so you don't have to "shoe horn" them in whenever you get a chance.

HOW TO AVOID GETTING SIDETRACKED BY INTERRUPTIONS

"Allowing the insistent demands of office life—interruptions, meetings, travel—to run unchecked is the surest way to negate all your planning and scheduling efforts." *Ibid.*, at 130. If this sounds like familiar story, you may not be working at peak efficiency because you're allowing your work time to become too fragmented. You will have to assert some control over how often and when you are interrupted in order to gain the benefits of an organized work schedule.

Yes, this is easier said than done. But there are several concrete steps you can take to reduce the frequency of interruptions and fragmented work time:

- set up interruption-free time periods, say 4:00 to 6:00 p.m. every day, and barring real emergencies, ask your secretary to hold calls and visitors

- instruct your secretary about the types of calls he or she can handle for you, and be sure to provide detailed instructions on how to handle them

- provide your secretary with a list of callers with whom you will always speak (your supervising attorney, an important client), and those for whom you would like messages taken

- consolidate all your telephone messages and return all non-priority calls at a specific time each day

- keep calls with long-winded callers brief by announcing at the beginning of the call, for example, that you only have five minutes available

- keep your office door closed during your private work time, or keep the door angled so you don't catch the eyes of pass-ersby

- consolidate visitor time by scheduling back-to-back meetings and appointments

- set limits on drop-by visitors—tell them you're in the middle of a priority project, ask if their questions can wait until you're free, or say you "can only give them five minutes because. . . ."

Use these (and other) methods to keep your work day organized, while remaining flexible enough to answer the needs of others, and also handle changes in your own workload.

USE MANAGEMENT STRUCTURES TO DEVELOP ORDERLY WORK PLANS

Some of the projects you'll be assigned will be very complex, involving several subtasks, tight scheduling and close monitoring. To handle these projects well, you need to develop a detailed plan for accomplishing the individual tasks and a method for monitoring progress.

Develop your overall plan first:

- set a goal: what is the purpose of the assignment?
- set a final deadline (if one has not already been set)
- break the project down into the steps required to meet your goal
- organize the subtasks into the order of performance
- set target dates for completion of each subtask
- delegate subtasks as appropriate (to your secretary and/or others)
- monitor everyone's progress until each goal is achieved and the project is completed

For instance, if your goal is to report back, in written form, to your supervising attorney on the steps required to file a RICO complaint for a client, the first step is to review the client file containing the facts of the matter. Next, conduct the required legal research, and confirm the continued validity of the case and statutory law your research turned up. Then ask your secretary (or the copy center) to photocopy the key cases and statutes the attorney might wish to review.

Now, you can prepare an outline of the legal memorandum you need to write. You draft the memorandum, your secretary types it, you review and revise the first draft and your secretary corrects it. Finally, you proofread the revised draft one more time and then your secretary prints the final version.

If you plan these steps ahead of time, notify the persons whose assistance you will need and set target dates for completion of each step, you will find that what may have seemed like a difficult task is in fact quite doable.

HOW TO CUT DOWN EXCESSIVE ADMINISTRATIVE TIME

You will always have some administrative, nonbillable time. What you want to do is keep this time down to what is truly necessary, so you can maximize your billable hours. How do you determine if your administrative time is excessive?

First, analyze your prior month's time records. Calculate the percentage of billable time to nonbillable time. If you're recording ten to fifteen percent administrative time, you're probably doing okay. Be sure to check with your supervising attorney, department manager or other policy maker. Some firms allow only five percent administrative time.

If you find that your percentage of administrative time is high, start keeping a work diary (if you're not doing so already for time billing). Track **all working time,** billable and nonbillable, and note at what time of the day you performed different tasks.

After collecting a few weeks of time in your work diary, go through it and highlight all the billable time in a particular color. Now, go through the diary and highlight your administrative time in another color. If you're working efficiently, and have consolidated all your administrative tasks, you will see broad bands of matching color. If not, you'll see a number of separate color stripes. Consolidating administrative tasks can reduce the time required to perform them.

Next, analyze the types of tasks you've highlighted as administrative time. Perhaps you should be **delegating** some of these tasks to your secretary or other support staff. You could also be **miscategorizing** time. Be sure to check with your supervising attorney about whether some of the time you've logged as administrative could really be billable time.

If you still have an excess of administrative time, the problem could be that you're accepting inappropriate assignments. You can easily remind the persons giving you assignments that your time should be billable. For example, ask for a billing number if you're asked to copy documents.

Remember, as a timekeeper in the firm, you will most likely have **a minimum billable hours requirement.** (*See* **Chapter Nine,** "Minimum Annual Billable Hours Requirements," for more on this issue.) If you accept assignments which cannot be billed, or perform work which you should delegate, you will be penalizing yourself, and denying your firm the revenue you were hired to produce.

Lawyers [and legal assistants] are intelligent people. Their lack of interest in management methods is not because of stupidity. They simply lack the knowledge of what systems and procedures can do for them in their law offices. They do not know how systems management can help them do their work faster and better, more economically for their clients, and, at the same time, increase their income, if that is their desire.

Altman & Weil, vii (from the "Preview" by K. Elson).

8

Time Billing
Management Reports

IMPORTANCE OF MONTH-END AND CUMULATIVE ANNUAL REPORTS

Monthly time reports allow the firm to ensure that all timekeepers are billing their time promptly, properly and that the annual budget for billable hours is being met. Annual reports provide information needed for performance evaluations, to assist with calculating future billable hours budgets, and forecasting the firm's revenue in the upcoming year. The following categories of information are ordinarily included in monthly and annual reports:

- total hours billed to clients for the year (or to date)
- total billable hours per month

- average billable hours per month
- total nonbillable hours for the year (or to date)
- total nonbillable hours per month
- average nonbillable hours per month
- total vacation/sick leave hours for the year (or to date)
- breakdowns of nonbillable hours into the following categories, usually in totals and averages per month:

>   office administration
>
>   pro bono
>
>   client development/marketing
>
>   recruiting activities
>
>   firm management/committees

- percentages of monthly and/or annual billable hours budgets met

See **Sample Timekeeper Reports 1, 2** and **3** for examples of different report formats.

REVIEW MONTH-END REPORTS TO CHECK FOR ACCURACY & CALCULATE EXPECTED ANNUAL TOTALS

Since firms' revenue projections are based on all timekeepers meeting their billable hours targets for each month and for the year, this is the most carefully scrutinized aspect of time reports. You can be sure that if your own monthly reports reflect below-budget billings, you will hear about it from your department manager or supervising attorney. This is why it's so important for you to track your own contributions to your firm's bottom line.

Sample Timekeeper Report # 1 is a "Month-End Time Category Breakdown" report dated 1/31/92. Because it's so early in the year, the total hours for the year to date are low. But you can still detect a number of interesting facts. Look at the top of the page: the billable hours for listed for timekeeper A equal only .75. Obviously, this person did not get his or her time records in by the cut-off date. (Most firms utilize a set time each month—a "cut-off date"—for receipt of all time sheets, so an orderly preparation of that month's client bills can begin.) This means that any work performed for clients by A during January will not be included in this month's client bills.

SAMPLE TIMEKEEPER REPORT 1
MONTH-END TIME CATEGORY BREAKDOWN

TOTAL as of 1/31/92

Timekeeper Name/Initials	Total Billable Hours	Nonbill. Hours	Office Admin.	Pro Bono	Vac/Sick Leave	Client Dev.	MONTHLY AVERAGES Billable	Nonbill.
A	.75	.00	.00	.00	.00	.00	.75	.00
B	105.00	22.50	7.50	15.00	.00	.00	105.00	7.50
C	236.75	5.00	.00	.00	.00	.00	236.75	5.00
D	203.25	30.25	11.75	.00	4.75	.00	203.25	16.50
E	124.75	8.00	.50	.00	7.50	.00	124.75	8.00
F	121.25	50.75	43.25	.00	7.50	.00	121.25	50.75
G	168.75	63.25	1.75	1.00	60.00	.00	168.75	63.25
H	89.00	37.50	.00	.00	37.50	.00	89.00	37.50
I	123.50	24.50	17.00	.00	7.50	.00	123.50	24.50
J	252.50	16.25	6.00	2.75	7.50	.00	252.50	16.25

You can see other interesting points, if you know where to look. Timekeeper B took some vacation time in January (15 hours), as did timekeepers F (7.50 hours), G (60 hours), H (37.50 hours), I (7.50 hours) and J (7.50 hours). Of course, this is not unusual for January.

What is unusual, and perhaps indicative of a potential problem, is the low billable hour total reported by timekeeper H. This person allocated 37.50 hours of vacation time, so this means he or she missed a week of billable time. But having only 89 billable hours for the rest of the month—for a total of 126.50 hours—is definitely too low by most firms' standards. If this trend continues (approximately 90 billable hours each month, or fewer than 1100 hours for the year), timekeeper H will not meet his or her billable hours budget, unless that budget has been set particularly low for some reason.

(Although your firm may differ, a majority of firms require between 1500 and 1800 billable hours per year. This translates into 125 and 150 billable hours per month, respectively. *See* **Chapter Nine** for a detailed discussion of minimum annual billable hours.)

There is one other point to note in **Sample Timekeeper Report # 1.** Look at the time reported by timekeeper J. This person obviously had a very busy month, billing 252.50 hours to clients. But note that he or she also broke out the nonbillable time very well. This time report—6 hours on office administration, 2.75 of pro bono work, and 7.50 hours of vacation time—shows good timekeeping habits.

Sample Timekeeper Report # 2, "Monthly Breakdown by Time-keepers Within Department," shows the time billing performances for all members in a single law firm department. The first thing you should notice is that the **percentage of billable time to nonbillable time,** while acceptable for January (85%), falls off significantly for February (73%) and March (74%).

SAMPLE TIMEKEEPER REPORT 2
MONTHLY BREAKDOWN BY TIMEKEEPERS WITHIN DEPARTMENT

TOTALS as of April 1992

Timekeeper Name/Initials	JANUARY Billable Hours	TOTAL Hours	FEBRUARY Billable Hours	Total Hours	MARCH Billable Hours	TOTAL Hours	AVERAGE MONTHLY BILLABLES
A	138.25	150.25	90.00	121.00	121.00	173.00	116.41
B	157.00	187.00	127.00	142.00	160.00	162.00	148.00
C	138.25	162.50	30.00	171.00	20.00	151.00	63.75
D	156.00	165.00	135.00	146.00	125.00	182.00	138.67
E	170.00	218.00	7.00	7.00	419.00	434.00	198.67
F	109.75	148.50	125.00	143.00	116.00	170.00	116.71
G	165.50	175.00	140.00	142.00	153.00	167.00	152.83
H	118.25	139.25	89.00	157.00	49.00	138.00	85.42
Averages	144.13	168.13	93.25	128.63	145.38	197.13	
Percentage of Billable Hours	85.7%		72.5%		73.7%		

This is primarily because one timekeeper, C, has reported only 33 and 20 billable hours for the last two months, while the nonbillable time worked remains quite high. Because in this report nonbillable time is not broken down into categories, there is no way of knowing if these hours constitute work on pro bono matters, or other justifiable use of nonbillable time.

You should also note that timekeeper E did not get his or her time sheets into the billing system by the cut-off date. This is obvious from the total of seven hours reported for February, and then 419 billable hours reported for March. This is **not** an acceptable practice, and should not be emulated.

Finally, **Sample Timekeeper Report # 3**, "Comparison to Budget & Projection of Annualized Totals," tracks the time for the same timekeepers shown in Sample Report # 2. Note that timekeepers B, D, E and G are right at or exceed their billable hours budgets for the year, which, in this example, is 1650 hours. Timekeepers A and F are within reach of their budgets, but timekeepers C and H have a long way to go to even come close.

SAMPLE TIMEKEEPER REPORT 3
COMPARISON TO BUDGET & PROJECTION OF ANNUALIZED TOTALS

TOTAL as of April 1992

Timekeeper Name/Initials	* Y-T-D Actual Billable Hours	Total Hours	** Y-T-D ANNUALIZED Billable Hours	Total Hours	*** % OF BUDGET Billable Hours	Total Hours
A	349.25	444.25	1,397	1,777	85%	99%
B	444.00	491.00	1,776	1,964	108%	109%
C	191.25	484.50	765	1,938	46%	108%
D	416.00	493.00	1,664	1,972	101%	109%
E	596.00	659.50	2,834	2,638	144%	147%
F	350.75	461.50	1,403	1,846	85%	102%
G	458.50	483.00	1,834	1,932	111%	107%
H	256.25	434.25	1,024	1,737	62%	96%

* Year to date totals for three months -- January, February & March.

** Annualized figures are derived from dividing year to date totals by 3 months, then multiplying by 12 to approximate annualized totals.

*** Percent of budget where annual budget for billable hours equals 1,650, & budget for total hours equals 1,800.

Each firm has its own form of month-end and annual time reports. The ones included here as examples may not look anything like the ones employed by your firm. Be sure to review your firm's reports with your department manager, supervising attorney or firm administrator.

You need to understand how to read these reports, and determine if any errors have been made. Because your performance evaluations will usually depend in large part on whether you have met the firm's minimum billable hour requirements (*see* **Chapter Nine** for more on this issue), you have a great stake in making sure these reports accurately reflect your work.

USE IN CREATING PREBILLS FOR BILLING ATTORNEY REVIEW

Different month-end time reports are generated for each client. These reports are sometimes used as draft bills for review by billing attorneys. Sometimes, though, special prebills are developed which show not only time records, but all cost expense items, such as photocopying, filing fees, and messenger costs, as well.

No matter what form these drafts or prebills take, the point is that your time records will be reviewed by that client's billing attorney in context with all other time billed to a particular client. It is at this point that questions about your time descriptions or about the amount of time reported for particular tasks may be raised. If you've been advising your supervising attorney of your progress, writing detailed time descriptions and allocating your time properly, chances are that the time you billed will make it past the billing attorney's review and actually be incorporated into the client's bill.

DIFFERENCES BETWEEN "WRITE OFFS" AND "WRITE DOWNS"

On the other hand, if there is some problem with your time billing, the client is particularly sensitive to expenses, the billing attorney is concerned with the total cost of the bill, or for any number of other reasons, your time may be reduced, that is, "written down." In particularly sensitive or difficult situations, your time may be deleted entirely, or "written off." Reductions in client bills are not always within your control, except for the way you keep time records and allocate your time in the first place.

While your time entries may survive the billing attorney's scrutiny, the client may later express concerns. Sometimes, if the firm believes the concerns are justified, or it simply wants to placate the client, the bill may be reduced after it has been sent to the client. Your time could also be written down or written off at this stage.

The only way you can influence whether your time gets past both hurdles is to keep detailed records, write detailed time descriptions, and allocate your time appropriately. If you do these things, you will have done your part to enhance the firm's revenues.

At Gordon & Rees, the firm encourages pro bono work but it is not part of the associates' 1,800-hour billable requirement.

At Hancock Rothert, the target for associates is 1,850 billable hours and hours clocked doing pro bono work count as part of that billable requirement.

Guynn, "Litigation Powerhouses Explain Their Successes," *California Law Business*, 14 (Daily Journal Corporation, Oct. 28, 1991).

The move to minimum hours opens the [corporate] law departments to a criticism historically directed at large law firms. "I think it's a fundamental mistake," says Hildebrandt's [Allen] Cleveland. "Rather than concentrate on the quality of work, you concentrate on the number of hours."

Varchaver, "Quantity Counts: the Push to Bill More Hours," *The American Lawyer*, 50 (Jan./Feb. 1992).

9

Minimum Annual Billable Hours Requirements

THE IMPORTANCE OF UNDERSTANDING YOUR FIRM'S MINIMUM BILLABLE HOURS REQUIREMENT

As illustrated by the first quotation at the beginning of this chapter, firms differ on what kinds of hours are counted toward the minimum billable target. In fact, some firms have real "requirements" for billable totals, while other employ mere "targets" for their timekeepers to reach. Some firms count pro bono hours or hours logged for client development as part of meeting the billable hours requirement. To other firms, "billable" hours means just that: only hours that are charged to clients and are thus likely to directly produce income are counted as "billable hours."

In order to know what billable hours standards your performance will be judged by, you must determine:

- whether the firm has strict requirements, or just a general target or goal for billable hours

- whether the firm employs different minimum requirements or targets for associates and legal assistants

- whether the firm requires higher billable hours for senior associates, while more junior attorneys and legal assistants have similar requirements

- to what extent meeting (or not meeting) the requirement/target amount is used in evaluating performance

- what weight is given to **achieving** the minimum requirement/target

- what weight is given to **surpassing** the minimum requirement/target

- whether the requirement/target amount is for total hours worked, or limited strictly client billable time

- what types of time are counted toward the billable hour total, i.e., pro bono efforts

- whether hours billed to work on the firm's in-house litigation or collections activities counts toward the minimum requirement/target

- under what circumstances, if any, may the minimum requirement/target be reduced or "forgiven," i.e., substantial work on firm committees, responsibility for recruiting or marketing efforts, etc.

- what "penalties," if any, exist if the minimum requirement/target is not met

Some firms have heeded the general advice that it is a mistake to concentrate solely on the number of hours billed. These firms endeavor to base performance evaluations primarily on the **quality** of your work, not merely the quantity. But subjective evaluations about whether someone is a "good" lawyer or legal assistant are much more difficult.

It's quite a bit easier to determine whether someone has met a simple objective standard like the number of hours billed. This is why in most firms, meeting or exceeding the minimum billable hours requirement (or target) has become the most important evaluation criteria.

WHAT IT MEANS IN TERMS OF SALARY INCREASES & BONUSES

Meeting or not meeting your firm's minimum billable hour requirements can have a significant impact on your compensation. Of course, to what extent your compensation is affected depends on how your firm views minimum hours. If the firm has a strict requirement for meeting the minimum billable hours, your compensation could be severely impacted if you do not meet this requirement. And this means you will receive a smaller raise and year-end bonus, if any.

If your firm looks primarily—or solely—to whether you have met the requirement, you could improve your compensation package significantly if you exceed the requirement. But keep in mind that in some firms, meeting the minimum requirement is viewed as billing just enough to get by. Or it may be viewed as only an average performance. In these settings, you must **exceed**—usually by a significant margin—the minimum requirement in order to have your performance in this category viewed as exceptional.

Sometimes, not meeting the minimum requirement can have dire consequences. In some firms, this could even mean losing your job, particularly if your firm is also considering ways to cut back on personnel and expenses, as so many firms have done in the early '90s. Absent these exigent circumstances, however, failing to meet the firm's expectations for billable hours may mean only that your position vis-a-vis your colleagues will not improve.

Remember, to some extent, you are competing with your colleagues. For associates, this is an obvious competition for partnership. For legal assistants, the competition may be less fierce, if only because the ultimate goal is less defined, but it still exists. One way firms can differentiate among competing peers is whether the minimum billable hours requirement or target has been met.

HOW TO TRACK MONTH-END TIME REPORTS TO MEET REQUIREMENTS

Sample Timekeeper Report # 3 (first introduced in **Chapter Eight,** and found at page 73), shows you one way to calculate your own projected annual totals for billable hours. Since this is a report for March, three months of billing activities have passed. In this example, if you add up all your billable time recorded for those three months, and divide by three, you'll get a monthly average. Now, multiply that average by twelve (months) to reach an expected total for the year.

Note that some firms multiply by only eleven months. This is because, due to vacation and holiday time off (usually two weeks and at least ten days, respectively), most timekeepers really work only eleven months in a year. Of course, if much sick time is used, the amount of available working time could be reduced even further.

Because of this allowed vacation, sick, and holiday time off, some firms use more sophisticated methods for calculating annualized billable hour totals. These calculations take into account the total amount of nonworking time allowed each timekeeper, and track that time off as the year goes by.

For example, if a timekeeper takes two weeks' vacation in March, his or her billable hours budget for that month is only half of what would be expected for these people **not** recording vacation time. In this way, timekeepers are not "penalized" in the sense of tracking their billable hours budgets simply because they might have taken a vacation early in the year.

Some firms have developed charts of how much billable time must be logged each month in order to meet the minimum requirement, and still take vacation, holidays, sick time. Of course, exactly how much billable time is required each month depends on the total amount required each year. For some firms, this ranges from 1500 hours for legal assistants to 1800 hours for associates. In other firms, no distinction is made between these two positions, and the same annual minimum requirement is employed. You will also find firms in which the minimum requirement is much higher—1950 to 2100 hours.

You should make sure you understand how your firm calculates annual billable hour requirements. You also need to understand how to read your firm's month-end time reports, and learn how to calculate your own expected annual billable hours totals. Remember, **you** are responsible for ensuring that you meet the billing requirements of your firm.

USE OF RANGES FOR BILLING RATES & IMPORTANCE OF TIME BEING BILLED AT APPROPRIATE RATE

Most firms now use a range of billing rates for associate attorneys and legal assistants. This means that as the timekeeper increases in experience and salary level, his or her billing rate also increases. Using a range of billing rates allows firms to keep salary levels commensurate with experience, while at the same time charging more for that experience and recovering more revenue.

If a flat billing rate were used across the board for a position, the firm would recover less in revenue for its most experienced staff, and obviously, this doesn't make sense. Sometimes, billing rates are set using the "rule of thirds." Firms using this approach generally set billing rates at a level that will allow them to allocate realized revenue as follows:

- one third for direct compensation costs, such as salary, bonus, and cost of benefits
- one third for indirect costs associated with employing persons in particular positions, such as secretarial assistance and office space (overhead)
- one third for profit

Thus, if a timekeeper's salary is $40,000, that person's hourly billing rate should be set at a level that will yield at least $120,000 in gross revenue. This would allow the firm to cover both direct and indirect costs, and still make a profit of $40,000. If the firm expected 1800 billable hours per year, setting this timekeeper's billing rate at $67 should yield $120,600 in gross billings.

As you can see from this example, firms must raise your billing rate as your salary increases in order to ensure profitability. If the market for your firm's services will not allow increasing billing rates, this can have a direct impact on salary increases. For example, if your firm is located in an area with a depressed economy, the firm may be constrained from increasing its hourly rates, and thus salaries.

Another way salaries can be affected by billing rates is whether the time billed is actually paid for by clients. Even though your billing rate is $80 per hour, the actual yield (or payment) for your time may only be $70 per hour. This lowered amount is called the "realization rate," which is what firms actually realize (collect) from their billings. If your realization rate is significantly lower than your billing rate, this will also affect the firm's profitability, and thus, its ability to give raises and bonuses.

When clients cannot pay their legal bills, the firm's revenues suffer. Sometimes the only solution is to decline further representation of financially unstable clients. "To a large extent, 'write downs' of standard rates and difficulties in collections [must] be offset by stricter client-selection procedures." Foster, ed., "Tougher Times Ahead Call for Cost Control Actions Now," *Law Office Management & Administration Report*, 18-19 (Apr. 1990).

Your firm's realization rate is almost wholly outside your control. How much the firm actually recovers for the amounts billed to clients depends on many factors, including the financial condition of the firm's clients. However, to the extent collections are reduced as a result of poor timekeeping habits and inadequate time descriptions, this is something you **can** control.

[T]he legal environment of the 1990s has unquestionably and radically changed. Demand for services is flattening—declining in some areas—and client resistance to fees and charges is stiffening. The volume of high-profit transactional matters and big-ticket real estate deals is now a tiny fraction of what it was some five years ago. And banks are more reluctant to lend to law firms than at any time in the past several decades.

"In Defense of Short-Term Strategies," *Law Office Management & Administration Report*, 2 (Oct. 1991).

———————————————10

Your Responsibilities as a Timekeeper

By now, you should know your responsibilities as a timekeeper. As someone who is at least partially responsible for the financial well being of your firm, you must take these responsibilities seriously, and develop good timekeeping habits. This is particularly true and important in today's vastly more competitive legal services market.

Just in case you need a final reminder, however, here is an abridged list of your responsibilities:

- record all your time
- bill your time **every** day
- write appropriate and detailed time descriptions
- bill time for those tasks authorized by your firm or the particular client involved

- avoid having time written off by billing attorneys (either at the prebill stage or in negotiation with clients over bills), by ensuring that the firm knows your time was well spent
- **always** ask the appropriate supervisor to find out firm policies on all timekeeping matters

Although you may not be responsible for the ultimate collection of fees, if your time is not being billed to or paid for by clients, you need to discover why, since this will affect the profitability of the firm, and ultimately your salary and/or bonus levels. It may be a situation wholly outside your control. Or it's possible that you can influence this issue by improving your timekeeping skills. If this is the case, you have a responsibility to make the appropriate adjustments.

Even though timekeeping is a responsibility, it also has its rewards. You will find that developing good timekeeping habits assists you in other areas of your work. You will be able to chart your growth as a legal professional. And, of course, you will also have the satisfaction of knowing that you have contributed to the financial welfare of your firm, which will ultimately inure to your benefit.

Suggested Additional Reading

1) "Where Did All the Billable Hours Go?" *Law Office Management & Administration Report*, 1, 15-16 (June 1992).

Henning was able to use case studies to prove that expert billers (even senior partners within the same firm) can differ by as much as 80% in the number of hours they capture out of the same situation. Henning's point: It's important for timekeepers not only to keep precise time records but to push for **written guidelines** that help all the lawyers [and legal assistants] in the firm accurately, consistently, and rationally record their time and expenses.

Ibid., quoting Joel Henning of Hildebrandt, Inc. (Chicago office) (emphasis added).

2) "Efficiency Audits," *California Lawyer*, 26 (May 1991)

3) Harris, "Firms Having to Adjust as Their Clients Cut Back," *California Law Business*, 8 (Daily Journal Corporation, Jan. 27, 1992)

A cottage industry has sprung up in the form of teams of insurance company lawyers evaluating legal fees to ferret out excessive charges and to crack down on abuses.

4) M. Altman & R. Weil, *How to Manage Your Law Office*, section 16.15 at 16-32 to 16-32.1 (Matthew Bender, rev. perm. ed. 1991) (hereinafter cited as "Altman & Weil").

The way in which fees are determined is moving full circle. Prior to the advent of time billing, many firms . . . considered the value or importance of the case to the client, the talent which would be required and for how long (most did not keep time records), the overall relationship with the client, the client's ability to pay, past experience with similar cases and various other subjective factors [in setting fees].

Law office management consultants . . . began to see that too many firms were placing themselves at an economic disadvantage . . . and began to advocate time recording and billing as an alternative . . . . Today, few lawyers . . . remember the day when they did not keep minute track of time spent on legal work.

By the end of the 80s, firms were looking for alternative billing methods to improve their profit picture.

See also Altman & Weil section 4.03 at 4-10.4; section 4.02 at 4-4 to 4-5.

5) "What Corporate Clients Are Now Demanding From Their Lawyers," *Law Office Management & Administration Report*, 3-6 (Oct. 1991).

6) Harris, "Halloran Strategy at BofA [Bank of America] Pays Dividends," *The Recorder*, 15 (Feb. 26, 1992)

> Halloran set a cap of $290 an hour on the base rates the bank would pay . . . .
> In addition, he told firms that if they want the banks' work they also will have to discount their rates across the board by at least 10 percent. No major California firm has refused, Halloran says.
> A few exceptions have been made where a firm could claim unique expertise. . . Halloran says BofA got its discounts without guaranteeing any minimum billings to firms.

7) Altman & Weil, section 11.04 at 11-17 to 11-18.

> One lawyer explained his reason for maintaining meticulous time records, although he very seldom based his bill directly on the time expended: "I keep time records for the same reason I wear glasses—I like to know where I've been."

8) Friedler & Prescott, "Associates Still Have Control of Their Destiny," *California Law Business*, 23 (Daily Journal Corporation, Feb. 24, 1992)

> Although there is hardly an associate [or legal assistant] who has not heard this on a weekly basis, it is crucial to keep accurate, timely, descriptive records of billable and non-billable time. This not only helps the firm to get out timely bills, it helps the lawyer [and legal assistant] to be organized in his or her practice.

9) Harris, "Halloran Strategy at BofA [Bank of America] Pays Dividends," *The Recorder*, 15 (Feb. 26, 1992)

> "I don't mind it too much," says one lawyer. "I worked 100 hours more last year. . . . What I do mind is that a large part of the department lies through its teeth" about hours. She says it is easy to pad because many divisions of the bank don't scrutinize the department's bills carefully.
> "There's certainly some sharp-pencil effect in the hours . . . [b]ut . . . line managers, who must pay in-house lawyers out of their operating budgets, will resist any padding . . . .

This Business of Confidentiality:

What Everyone Doesn't Need to Know

By Jill S. Levin, Esq.
and
Dana L. Graves

Publisher's Note

This Business of Confidentiality contains suggestions to help you follow the ethical requirements to keep all client information confidential. It is **not** meant to replace any policy, procedures or any other guidelines your firm may have. Be sure to review your firm's employee handbook, if any, and check with all appropriate personnel for specific guidance concerning your firm's requirements and expectations on these issues.

Introduction

The importance of being ever vigilant in the protection of a client's confidentiality is well illustrated by the following true story.

Once, on a large case involving multiple parties, a third party in the matter had scheduled a document production at the site of the company's offices. Representatives for both the plaintiff and defendant had to be present to oversee the course of discovery. It just so happened that the chosen representatives had not met before, and so did not know each other by sight.

The defendant's legal assistant arrived at the company's offices early and took a seat in the reception area. She began reviewing her notes while waiting for the document production to begin. Shortly thereafter, an associate attorney and a paralegal from the plaintiff's law firm showed up and were also shown to the reception area to wait.

As time passed, the associate and paralegal began discussing some particular aspects of the plaintiff's case. The associate detailed the firm's strategy in requesting these particular documents from the third party, what they hoped to show, and generally how the plaintiff's case was proceeding. This discussion took place freely in front of the legal assistant who was there to represent the defendant in the pending litigation.

This attentive legal assistant began taking notes of the conversation between the attorney and paralegal for the plaintiff. There was no concern displayed by the participants that their conversation could be overheard, and they continued to discuss the plaintiff's strategy at length. All this time, the defendant's legal assistant continued to take notes, while trying to appear as if she was not paying attention to the very revealing conversation.

Finally, after a wait of about 30 minutes, the third party's lawyer walked into the reception room. She approached the plaintiff's and defendant's representatives, greeting them with: "Good, you've already met each other. Shall we get started?"

Imagine the look on the associate's face when he realized that he'd been discussing the firm's strategy for the litigation and other confidential aspects of the case in front of the opposition.

As a result of this breach of confidentiality, the plaintiff fired the firm it had been using for this matter and later sued for malpractice. The associate involved was terminated for this gross violation of the client's confidences, and although the paralegal was merely reprimanded, her career was still damaged. On the other hand, the legal assistant for the defendant's law firm was roundly congratulated on her perspicacity and for quickly taking advantage of this situation.

Maintaining the confidentiality of all client matters is crucial to attorneys and the practice of law. Employees, agents and independent contractors—that is, anyone working for attorneys, whether in law firms, corporations or legal services programs—**must** carefully observe this duty of confidentiality.

Why is confidentiality so crucial?

Fostering a good relationship with clients is certainly economically beneficial to a law practice, but the rules regarding confidentiality are based on more important principles. For attorneys to provide the best advice and counsel, all information pertinent to a case or matter must be made available to them. Clients often need to confide personal or even intimate information. They may also need to provide information that is damaging to a legal claim or defense. As a result, clients must feel secure that all this necessary information will be kept confidential.

Courts have long recognized this dual need for information and confidentiality:

> While it is the great purpose of law to ascertain the truth, there is the countervailing necessity of insuring the right of every person to freely and fully confer and confide in one having knowledge of the law, and skilled in its practice, [so] that the former may have adequate advice and proper defense. This assistance can be made safely and readily available only when the client is free from the consequences of apprehension of disclosure by reason of the subsequent statements of the skilled lawyer.

Baird v. Koerner, 279 F.2d 623, 629-30 (9th Cir. 1960).

Many do not realize that the attorney is in fact the **agent** of the client. The client is the one who solicits and employs an attorney. Ultimately, it is the client who has the final decision-making power to settle a lawsuit or go to trial, for example. This is true even though the attorney is the specialist, the expert in the field of law whose education, experience and expertise is required. (*See* **Appendix** for American Bar Association Model Rule 1.2, discussing "Scope of Representation.")

As an agent, the attorney owes not only a **duty of care** and a **duty of loyalty** to the client, additional ethical requirements apply. The **duty of confidentiality** is primary among these. This duty encompasses the requirement to carefully guard the confidences, secrets and "privileged" information communicated to the attorney by the client or on the client's behalf. (*See* **Appendix** for American Bar Association Model Rule 1.7, "Conflict of Interest," specifying the lawyer's duty of loyalty to the client.)

Traditionally, attorneys practiced independently or in a small partnership with only the support of a legal secretary or sometimes a law clerk. Obviously, under these circumstances, observing the duty of confidentiality was much simpler.

Today, however, that picture has changed considerably. Although the majority of attorneys still practice independently or in small firms, the practice of law has grown and changed to such an extent that there are several large law firms of over 100 attorneys (and even a few firms of over 1,000 attorneys). Additionally, corporate law departments, legal services programs and thousands of government attorneys function in a myriad of agencies and departments. Attorneys have never been more specialized than they are today.

With more attorneys practicing law in so many different areas, and in so many different organizations, attorneys have discovered that they cannot effectively handle their clients' affairs without a host of new personnel to assist them, given the complexities of the modern law practice. Today, the average attorney not only utilizes the services of a legal secretary, but almost certainly also employs a legal assistant, calendar clerk, word processor and messenger.

Outside legal services vendors such as investigators, printers, and photocopying shops are commonly used. Today's law practice also requires the use of numerous experts, including accountants, physicians and engineers. In *United States v. Kovel*, 296 F.2d 918, 921 (2d Cir. 1961), the court, in deciding that an accountant's services — solicited by an attorney for his client — were protected confidential communications and need not be disclosed, also acknowledged that few lawyers could practice without the help of others.

We now live in a fast-paced, information-rich, but time-poor society. Attorneys are confronted daily with more information from more sources than they can assimilate. This "information explosion" has resulted in a vast number of new information sources and created mountains of documents that must be reviewed and digested.

- One hundred years ago, offices began using manual typewriter. The telephone was just around the corner. Computers, photocopying machines and facsimile machines were not yet dreamed of.

- Fifty years ago, the storage requirements for a single computer took up an entire room. Telephones carried only one line.

- Now, the typewriter has been replaced by a personal computer. PCs are equipped for handling word processing, time and billing functions and gaining access to extensive databases. They can be networked with other computers in one or many offices. Telephone systems now offer such popular features as voice-mail, teleconferencing and call forwarding; they can also be programmed to bill clients. Car phones, mobile telephones and coast-to-coast video teleconferencing are making inroads.

Clearly, attorneys cannot meet with clients; conduct research; draft documents; consult with staff, colleagues or opposing counsel; or appear at depositions and in court, if they must also closely monitor and manage all law office personnel and equipment.

As a result, information that was once only communicated to (and known by) the attorney and a trusted legal secretary, may now be available to the attorney's entire staff. With a larger staff and expanding use of technology, the attorney's responsibility for maintaining client confidentiality has become more difficult.

All these factors—the advances in technology, the growing complexity of the law, and the changing nature of the organizations in which law is practiced—highlight the real need for understanding the requirements for confidentiality. And all those associated with the practice of law—as attorneys, legal assistants, support staff, consultants and service providers—must address their individual obligations.

This Business of Confidentiality: What Everyone Doesn't Need to Know provides a much-needed foundation for understanding the scope of confidentiality requirements. It also describes the practical boundaries for ensuring client confidentiality in day-to-day work.

1

History and Codification of Confidentiality Requirements

WHAT STANDARDS GOVERN CONFIDENTIALITY?

Attorneys must be licensed by each state in which they seek to practice law. Upon being licensed, they must swear that they will follow all ethical guidelines, state rules and regulations governing their profession. Legal assistants and paralegals are also bound by ethical guidelines, although there is currently no legal requirement—or enforcement—of compliance. On the other hand, most support staff are not subject to any specifically tailored informal or legal requirements.

However, all employees, agents, independent contractors and others engaged by attorneys to perform particular tasks or services **are** bound, in effect, by the rules which govern attorneys.

The basic outlines of these rules and guidelines are set forth below. While attorneys will be intimately familiar with these strictures, people new to the legal profession are not. Although each state may use somewhat different language in its regulations, the general guidelines governing a lawyer's professional behavior are quite similar from state to state.

Regulation by the States

Since the practice of law affects the public interest, each state exercises jurisdiction over attorneys practicing within the state and thus regulates the legal profession's relationship with its clients. Because the administration of justice is overseen by courts, the ultimate power to regulate the legal profession resides with the courts, particularly the highest court of each state. The New Mexico Supreme Court noted the importance of this responsibility, stating: "The canons of professional ethics must be enforced by the Courts and must be respected by members of the Bar if we are to maintain public confidence in the integrity and impartiality of the administration of justice." *In re Meeker*, 76 N.M. 354, 357, 414 P.2d 862, 864 (1966).

Another, powerful source of regulation comes from each state's bar association, which receives, investigates and acts on complaints regarding attorneys. (Note that attorneys are uniformly required to be members of their respective state bar associations, although membership in the American Bar Association (ABA) is voluntary.) In addition, state legislatures regularly pass statutes affecting attorney conduct, especially concerning admission to the bar and the regulation of legal fees. Thus, attorneys' conduct is regulated not only through the courts and state bar associations, but also through statutes, preexisting case law, rules governing attorney appearances in court and rules of ethical conduct.

State bar associations are also charged with actually administering and overseeing the admission of law school graduates to practice law. In conjunction with passing a state's bar exam, most candidates for the bar must also pass the Multi-State Professional

Responsibility Examination (MPRE). Before being admitted to the bar, a number of states first require candidates to have reached a certain age, to have graduated from an ABA-accredited law school and to have good moral character.

The MPRE covers three topics: the professional conduct of lawyers, the professional conduct of judges and the law of legal malpractice. Courses in "Professional Responsibility" are required courses in most law schools. Many states now also mandate that attorneys take a minimum number of hours of continuing legal education to maintain their good standing as active attorneys. California, for instance, recently instituted a Mandatory Continuing Legal Education (MCLE) program. This program requires attorneys to take a total of 36 hours of classes during a period of three years. Eight out of the required 36 hours must be dedicated solely to ethics.

In most states, the genesis of these rules of conduct is the ABA Model Rules concerning ethics. The ABA is the largest and most outspoken nationwide organization of lawyers. Although having substantially less than half the nation's attorneys as members, the ABA often casts itself as the national voice of the legal profession. Primary ABA functions include:

- providing continuing legal education,

- creating and interpreting model rules of ethics for lawyers and judges,

- coordinating committees oriented to practice specializations,

- making recommendations about persons proposed for federal judgeships, and

- supporting or opposing legislation that may affect the practice of law and the administration of justice.

Regulation by the American Bar Association

The ABA first issued its **Canons of Professional Ethics** in 1908. In 1969, the ABA drafted and adopted its **Model Code of Professional Responsibility** ("Model Code") and in 1983 it replaced the

Model Code with the **Model Rules of Professional Conduct** ("Model Rules"). Before the existence of the Model Rules, most states had adopted, in large part, the Model Code of Professional Conduct. Now, however, most states have replaced the Model Code with the Model Rules. *See* Elliot, "With Whom May I Talk and What May I Say? Current Issues in Legal Ethics," 65 *Conn. B. J.* 81, 83 (Apr. 1991).

A few states adopted neither the Model Code nor the Model Rules. Instead, these states codified and drafted individual state codes of attorney conduct. In California, for example, ethical behavior is generally governed by the Rules of Professional Conduct of the State Bar of California and the State Bar Act. *See* Cal. Bus. & Prof. Code §§ 6000-6228 (West 1988).

The 1969, the ABA Model Code consisted of nine general statement of rules concerning ethics, referred to as "Canons." Each Canon is followed by Ethical Considerations ("ECs") and Disciplinary Rules ("DRs"), both of which interpret and/or mandate required behavior. The Canons, enumerated below, neatly identify key ethical concerns facing attorneys then and today. These basic guidelines, reinterpreted in the Model Rules, carry over, in some form, into each state's rules of conduct.

Canon 1 A Lawyer Should Assist in Maintaining the Integrity and Competence of the Legal Profession.

Canon 2 A Lawyer Should Assist the Legal Profession in Fulfilling Its Duty to Make Legal Counsel Available.

Canon 3 A Lawyer Should Assist in Preventing the Unauthorized Practice of Law.

Canon 4 A Lawyer Should Preserve the Confidences and Secrets of a Client.

Canon 5 A Lawyer Should Exercise Independent Professional Judgment on Behalf of a Client.

Canon 6 A Lawyer Should Represent a Client Competently.

Canon 7 A Lawyer Should Represent a Client Zealously Within the Bounds of the Law.

Canon 8 A Lawyer Should Assist in Improving the Legal System.

Canon 9   A Lawyer Should Avoid Even the Appearance of
Professional Impropriety.

With the increasing acceptance and growth of the paralegal
profession, in 1991, the ABA issued its "Model Guidelines for the
Utilization of Legal Assistant Services." These Guidelines were
intended primarily for attorneys, and they include parallel direc-
tives to those found in the ABA Model Rules.

> **Guideline 1**: A lawyer is responsible for all of the professional
> actions of a legal assistant performing legal assistant services
> at the lawyer's direction and should take reasonable measures
> to ensure that the legal assistant's conduct is consistent with
> the lawyer's obligations under the ABA Model Rule of Profes-
> sional Conduct.

> **Guideline 2**: Provided the lawyer maintains responsibility for
> the work product, a lawyer may delegate to a legal assistant any
> tasks normally performed by the lawyer except those tasks
> proscribed to one not licensed as lawyer by statute, court rule,
> administrative rule or regulation, controlling authority, the
> ABA Model Rules of Professional Conduct, or these Guidelines.

In 1988, the National Association of Legal Assistants, Inc.
("NALA") and the National Federation of Paralegal Associations
("NFPA"), both national organizations, adopted their own guide-
lines of conduct for paralegals. *See* NALA's "Code of Ethics and
Professional Responsibility," and NFPA's "Affirmation of Respon-
sibility." *See also* a new book addressing the role of paralegals,
Ethics and Professional Responsibility for Legal Assistants, by Therese A.
Cannon (Little, Brown and Company, 1992).

Repercussions for Breaches of Conduct by Attorneys

Disciplinary proceedings are not lawsuits between parties, but
rather are inquiries into the conduct of attorneys. The purpose of
such proceedings is not punishment. Instead, these proceedings
seek to determine the "fitness" of an attorney to continue practicing law. *In re Echeles*, 430 F.2d 347, 349 (7th Cir. 1970). The
underlying purpose, of course, is to protect the courts and the
public from attorneys unfit to practice law. The ABA "Standards

for Lawyer Discipline and Disability Proceedings" (approved in 1979, and amended in 1983), state:

> **1.1. Purpose of Lawyer Discipline and Disability Proceedings.**
> The purpose of lawyer discipline and disability proceedings is to maintain appropriate standards of professional conduct in order to protect the public and the administration of justice from lawyers who have demonstrated by their conduct that they are unable or are likely to be unable to properly discharge their professional duties.

When attorneys allegedly violate a rule of professional ethics, they may be faced with professional disciplinary proceedings. Typically, when the state bar receives a complaint from an aggrieved person, the bar association investigates the complaint to determine if the complaint has merit. If so determined, the bar association will then set a date for hearing evidence. Usually, a panel of attorneys from the community will preside at the hearing. At the conclusion of the hearing, the panel makes a recommendation for action by the state bar. The panel's finding may be that the attorney has not breached any ethical duty, and therefore, no action need be taken.

In most states, the bar association is responsible for meting out appropriate punishment when an attorney has been found by the panel to have breached a rule of conduct. Where a lesser breach of duty is found, the panel can recommend censure or reprimand. The attorney then receives a public or private admonition declaring the behavior at issue improper. This type of admonition does **not** limit the attorney's right to practice law. Disciplinary proceedings may also result in other remedies, such as ordering the attorney to enter a substance abuse program, make restitution of a client's misappropriated funds or other measures tailored to the situation.

More egregious breaches of conduct can result in an attorney being prohibited from practicing law for a specified period, commonly referred to as being "suspended" from practice. The most severe discipline that can be meted out is "disbarment." Once disbarred, an attorney can never again practice law in that state. Cases of disbarment can be reviewed by one or more state courts, but generally, the power to disbar an attorney is held exclusively by the state bar associations.

Repercussions for Breaches of Conduct by Nonlawyers

The ethical rules referred to above "define the type of ethical conduct that the public has the right to expect not only of lawyers but **also of their non-professional employees and associates** in all matters pertaining to professional employment." This is stated in the "Preamble and Preliminary Statement" of the ABA Model Code.

Today's practice of law usually requires the participation of any number of other employees or independent contractors to prosecute, defend or otherwise complete a transaction, such as a will, real estate closing or contract for the sale of a business. For purposes of this monograph, "independent contractors" refers to all those individuals or companies who, while performing services at the direction of the attorney, are not full-time employees. Some independent contractors commonly used by law firms include investigators, accounting services, expert witnesses, real estate appraisal companies and printing services.

The attorney, of course, is bound by the all the rules and regulations previously mentioned. And even though it may sometimes be difficult for attorneys to manage just their own business and ethical affairs, attorneys are also responsible for the ethical standards of their staff. Should a member of the attorney's staff breach an ethical rule, particularly the rules governing client confidentiality, it is the attorney who will suffer professionally.

An employee or independent contractor may jeopardize the success of a client's case if information is improperly disclosed. This could potentially force the attorney to resign from a matter, cause the attorney to lose fees, harm the attorney's professional reputation or cause other sanctions to be suffered. Needless to say, an employee or independent contractor of a firm who does disclose confidential information may also suffer the consequences of such action, including termination of employment.

Thus, it is **everyone's duty** to maintain the confidentiality about a client's representation and any information provided in connection with that representation. This applies not only **during** the term of your employment, but even **after** your employment ends. Once you sign a confidentiality agreement, this obligation continues forever, just as it does for attorneys.

PROHIBITIONS AGAINST INSIDER TRADING

As detailed above, ethical rules barring the use of confidential information primarily govern attorneys' behavior. Violations of these rules can result in sanctions against attorneys, even though the breach may have occurred as a result of an employee's mistake or action. Thus, the toughest "penalty" that can be applied to any employee involved in an ethical violation is termination of employment.

But there are also federal laws prohibiting the use of confidential — or "inside" — information to gain a financial advantage. The strict laws forbidding the use of inside information apply to **all** people with access to such information, and the penalties for violation of the laws apply across the board as well.

What Is "Inside" Information?

To obtain financing, a corporation typically issues "securities." A security can be defined as any document reflecting either a debt or a property interest in the entity issuing the security. From the investor's standpoint, a security is an investment in an enterprise, from which the investor expects profits to be derived through the efforts of those running the entity.

Although securities can take many forms, they most commonly fall into two categories: "stocks" and "bonds." In purchasing stocks, the stock owner buys an equity interest in the corporation. This interest entitles the owner to participate in corporate earnings, if any, and in the distributions of corporate trusts or other property. On the other hand, bonds are a type of debt. Bonds represent the corporation's obligation to repay money to the holders of the bonds.

Potential investors in a corporation obviously must investigate the benefits and risks involved in making these kinds of investments. But, to keep the playing field level, and to make the investment risks fair to all, investors are limited to information that is generally available to or known by the public at large.

Occasionally, however, some investors will gain an advantage over other investors, thus reducing their risk, by obtaining information which is not available to the public. This nonpublic, "inside" information, is information which is known only by a limited group of people somehow affiliated with the corporation. Investments based on inside information are unethical and illegal.

Laws Governing the Use of Inside Information

The Securities Exchange Act of 1933 (15 U.S.C. §§ 77a-77aa), and later, the Securities Exchange Act of 1934 (15 U.S.C. §§ 77a-78jj; hereinafter referred to the "1934 Act"), were enacted to prevent fraud and stabilize the securities industry. These federal statutes required that specific information about the risks and basis for each investment must accompany the issuance of securities. They also established mechanisms to oversee the resale of securities by national security exchanges, brokers and dealers, and national securities associations, such as the National Association of Securities Dealers (NASD). As a result, the sale of securities by public corporations is heavily regulated.

One of the most important areas of the 1934 Act relates to "insider trading." (Section 10(b) and Rule 10b-5 of the 1934 Act address this problem.) The 1934 Act prohibits corporate directors and officers—the "corporate insiders"—from taking financial advantage of information which was obtained because of their unique positions. Because this information may have substantial impact on the future market value of corporate securities, it provides these individuals a distinct advantage over the unknowing persons with whom they deal.

The application of this "anti-insider trading" rule has been extended to all others who may receive inside information from a corporation's director or officer. It also applies to others who are in a position to misappropriate such information.

The theory of liability for misappropriation holds that an individual who obtains inside information and trades on it for personal gain could be held liable for "stealing" such information. *See, e.g., Chiarella v. United States*, 445 U.S. 222 (1980), in which an outside printer (working for the corporation who determined the unidentified corporate target of a takeover bid was not held liable as "insider". Under a subsequent theory of misappropriation, however, the printer Chiarella might not have escaped liability. In *United States v. Carpenter*, 791 F.2d 1024 (2d Cir. 1986), a reporter for the *Wall Street Journal* and others were found liable for entering into a scheme to use advance, nonpublic, and material information which came from corporate officers who provided it to the reporter for use in future columns.

Obligations of Law Firms and Firm Employees

By the very nature of legal work, attorneys, legal assistants and nonlawyer personnel may become privy to inside information. Of course, both the insider trading laws and the ethical rules governing confidentiality restrict the use of this information. However, a violation of the insider trading laws can result in both monetary and criminal penalties being imposed.

Thus, while a breach of confidentiality may result in a reprimand to the nonlawyer employee or the loss of employment, if inside information was involved, being found guilty of violating federal securities laws carries a much heavier penalty. This is true both for the individual involved and the firm.

For example, if a legal assistant learns that a real estate development being handled by a firm will result in dramatic increases in property values in the surrounding areas, the legal assistant should not misuse this information to buy property. . . . In addition to the individual's liability under securities law, the firm [may also be found] liable. Under the Insider Trading and Securities Fraud Enforcement Act of 1988, . . . fines of up to $1 million may be levied against a law firm whose employee uses confidential or inside information to engage in unlawful securities transactions if the firm did not exercise appropriate supervision to prevent the unlawful trading.

T. CANNON, ETHICS AND PROFESSIONAL RESPONSIBILITY FOR LEGAL ASSISTANTS 101-02 (1992) (citing 15 U.S.C. § 78 (1988)).

The significance of this issue has not been overlooked by many law firms, who have developed in-house training programs and written policies for inclusion in employee manuals. Some bar associations have also recently reviewed and drafted model policy statements regarding these issues. *See, e.g.,* Los Angeles County Bar Ass'n, REPORT ON LAW FIRM POLICIES RELATING TO CONFIDENTIALITY AND SAFEGUARDING INSIDE INFORMATION (1985).

2

Requirements for Attorney Supervision

RESPONSIBILITY FOR SUPERVISING NONLAWYER PERSONNEL

The Preamble to the ABA Model Code states that: "A lawyer should ultimately be responsible for the conduct of his employees and associates in the course of the professional representation of the client." From this and the following discussion, we learn that:

- A nonlawyer is entitled to instruction on ethical issues.

- The attorney is under a duty to provide such instruction.

- The nonlawyer's work is to be supervised by the attorney.

■ The attorney must assume complete professional responsibility for the work product of nonlawyers.

■ The attorney's failure to supervise may result in disciplinary action against the attorney.

Under these guidelines, an attorney would be remiss if he or she did not provide some **ethical instruction** to staff members (or independent contractors), or **failed to supervise** the performance of work delegated to nonlawyer employees.

Obligation to Provide Instruction Regarding Ethics

Frequently, instruction regarding ethical obligations occurs when the new employee begins work. New associates may not be included because most have already taken mandatory law school courses in "Professional Responsibility." Unfortunately, outside investigators, accountants or other consultants sometimes never receive any instruction at all. In addition, this responsibility may be delegated to the office manager, or it may simply consist of a "conflicts check" (discussed later in this Chapter), to ensure that the new employee does not jeopardize any present or future matters to be handled by the attorney. Additional instruction usually occurs, at best, on an ad hoc basis.

The Comments following Model Rule 5.3 note that lawyers generally employ secretaries, clerks, investigators, law students and legal assistants. These Comments also note that whether these people are employees or independent contractors, the "lawyers should give such assistants appropriate instruction and supervision concerning the ethical aspects of their employment, **particularly regarding the obligation not to disclose information relating to representation of the client.**" MODEL RULES OF PROFESSIONAL CONDUCT Rule 5.3 comment (1983) (emphasis added) (hereinafter cited as "Model Rules").

Obligation to Supervise Delegated Work

The problems involved in delegating work to nonlawyers and supervising their performance are addressed specifically in Ethical Consideration 3-6 of the Model Code. This section states that delegation of client work "is proper if the lawyer maintains a direct relationship with [the] client, supervises the delegated work, and has complete professional responsibility for the work product." MODEL CODE OF PROFESSIONAL RESPONSIBILITY EC 3-6 (1980) (hereinafter cited as "Model Code"). Further, the Disciplinary Rules address the issue of confidentiality:

> A lawyer shall exercise reasonable care to prevent his employees, associates, and others whose services are utilized by him from **disclosing or using confidences** or secrets of a client, except that a lawyer may reveal the information allowed by DR 4-101(C) through an employee.

MODEL CODE DR 4-101 (D) (1980).

Similarly, ABA Model Rule 5.3 (set forth in full in the **Appendix**), mandates attorney supervision of nonlawyer employees. The partner or supervisory attorney in a law firm, business entity, governmental unit or legal services office must "make **reasonable** efforts to ensure that the person's conduct is compatible with the professional obligations of the lawyer." The failure to instruct and/or supervise nonlawyer personnel may subject the attorney to professional discipline. *See, e.g., Crane v. State Bar*, 30 Cal. 3d 117, 177 Cal. Rptr. 670, 672, 635 P.2d 163, 165 (1981).

This Rule substantially parallels Model Rule 5.1. As outlined in Rule 5.1 (discussed in detail below), partners and other lawyers with direct supervisory authority over other lawyers must make reasonable efforts to ensure that the lawyers in the firm (or the lawyer directly supervised), conform to the rules of professional conduct.

While it is clear that nonlawyer employees are not subject to the ethical rules and standards required of lawyers, the attorney has long been held responsible for the work of his or her employees. In *Vaughn v. State Bar*, 6 Cal. 3d 847, 100 Cal. Rptr. 713, 494 P.2d 1257 (1972), a problem arose when a member of an attorney's support staff failed to inform him that certain funds had been received. The court still found the attorney at fault. "[E]ven though an attorney cannot be held responsible for every detail of office procedure, he must accept responsibility [for] supervis[ing] the work of his staff." 494 P.2d at 1263.

This does **not** mean, however, that the attorney will automatically held liable for the wrongful acts of nonlawyers. Nor is the attorney required to guarantee the conduct of the nonlawyer. Attorneys will generally be found **not** liable for the acts of nonlawyers **unless** the attorney had failed to take any precautionary steps.

In a similar vein, according to Model Rule 5.3(c), attorneys must not order or sanction the breach of professional ethics by others. However, it will generally be considered a violation of this ethical rule if the supervising attorney knows "of the conduct at a time when its consequences can be avoided or mitigated but fails to take reasonable remedial action."

SUPERVISORY RESPONSIBILITY FOR OTHER ATTORNEYS

Just as an attorney is generally accountable for nonlawyer personnel, partners or supervisory attorneys may also be held responsible for the attorneys working under their direction or control. Model Rule 5.1, "Responsibility of a Partner or Supervisory Lawyer," declares that supervisory attorneys must take reasonable steps to ensure that all attorneys under their direction follow the rules of professional conduct. (*See* **Appendix** for the full text of this rule.) These obligations bind attorneys working in law firms as well as in corporate law departments and governmental agencies.

The definition of "reasonable measures" varies, depending on the nature, structure and size of the firm. Partners or supervisory attorneys in a small firm may find that informal instruction or reprimands may satisfy the reasonableness requirement. On the other hand, larger firms may require more formal structures to handle ethical problems, since larger firms may encounter complex ethical issues more often.

An independent duty of supervision must be established. The partner or supervisory attorney is responsible for the acts of other attorneys when he or she:

■ has ordered the conduct complained of, "or with knowledge of the specific conduct, ratifies the conduct involved," or

■ has "direct supervisory authority over the other lawyer, and knows of the conduct at a time when its consequences" could have been avoided or mitigated, but fails to do so.

Model Rule 5.1, therefore, does not impose disciplinary liability upon a supervisory attorney who has not participated in or ratified a violation of the Model Rules.

Of course, a subordinate lawyer is not immune from professional responsibility. Model Rule 5.2, "Responsibilities of a Subordinate Lawyer," require adherence to the rules of professional conduct despite the fact that "the lawyer acted at the direction of another person." (*See* **Appendix** for full text of Model Rule 5.2.) However, where the subordinate attorney's action is in accordance with a supervisory attorney's "reasonable resolution of an arguable question of professional duty," the subordinate will not be found to have violated the rules of professional conduct.

These Model Rules manifest both the oversight responsibilities of senior attorneys, as well as each individual attorney's responsibility for his or her own professional conduct.

ANALYSIS OF PARTICULAR SITUATIONS

Changing Employment

A case typifying the application of ethical rules when an employee changes jobs follows. A secretary, Sarah, changed employment and began working for a second law firm. As it happens, Sarah's former employer and her new one represented clients who opposed each other in a law suit. In fact, Sarah actually worked on the matter in question for the plaintiff at her old law firm and now has begun working on the same matter for the defendant at the new firm. The plaintiff seeks to have the defendant's law firm disqualified from continuing to represent the defendant because of Sarah's involvement in the matter.

The following facts greatly affected the outcome of the disqualification hearing. At her former firm, Sarah had been given relatively insignificant duties, and most of the case preparation was completed before Sarah began working at that firm. In addition, Sarah provided no confidential information to her new firm, and this new firm had specifically instructed Sarah not to discuss her knowledge of the case.

In this instance, the new employer was found to have properly instructed the employee not to disclose any confidential information to which she may have had access. The new firm, which represented the defendant, was not forced to withdraw from representing its client. *Esquire Care, Inc. v. Maguire*, 532 So. 2d 740 (1988).

A starkly different result occurred in another case involving a law firm employee who changed jobs. In this instance, the employee was a paralegal. The courts ruled in favor of the defendant's motion for disqualification of a plaintiff's firm because the plaintiff firm hired an experienced paralegal who had previously worked on quite similar asbestos cases for the defense side. For more details on this case from California, *see* discussions concerning nonlawyer employees in **Chapter 4** (under "Screening Potential Employees for Conflicts of Interest" and "Analysis of Particular Situations").

Sharing Office Space and Services

Attorneys sharing offices is a common situation, particularly for small firms and sole practitioners. In one such case, two attorneys had each rented space in a suite owned by a third attorney. A secretary employed by the first of the renting attorneys was frequently asked to assist the second attorney, who paid the first attorney for all secretarial services provided.

In the course of the legal secretary's "dual" employment, the secretary divulged to the second attorney some key information regarding a competitive property bid that was prepared for the first attorney and the attorney who owned the office. Apparently, there was no plan or effort on the part of second attorney to procure this information, and the secretary's disclosure was deemed unintended or accidental.

In an advisory opinion prepared by the California Committee on Professional Responsibility and Conduct, each of the attorneys was considered to be under an obligation to prevent the disclosure of information. This obligation applied to all three attorneys, since each one benefitted from the shared office and shared secretary arrangement.

The first attorney, the one who had originally hired the secretary, should have properly defined the secretary's obligations with respect to confidentiality and employment by the other attorneys. Similarly, the other attorneys should have discussed this issue with the secretary and with the first attorney before hiring the secretary to prepare the bid.

The opinion of the Committee, although advisory, recommended that the attorneys disclose this breach of confidentiality to their clients. The attorneys were also advised to withdraw from further representation of the parties concerning the property at issue. Cal. Comm. on Prof. Resp. & Conduct, Formal Op. 1979-50.

Using Outside Services

Attorneys frequently need to use outside services such as printers, bookkeepers, graphics companies and copy services. When these engagements involve disclosing confidential client information, the attorney must:

- properly select the outside service,

- warn the people involved in the project about the confidential nature of their work, and

- ascertain that the outside services have appropriate internal rules in place to maintain the confidentiality of the information conveyed.

When these steps have been followed, no ethical improprieties in sharing the amount of confidential information required for the services to perform its job will ordinarily be found.

Model Code Ethical Consideration 4-3 specifically addresses such situations:

Unless the client otherwise directs, it is not improper for a lawyer to give limited information from his file to an outside agency necessary for statistical bookkeeping, accounting, data processing, banking, printing, or other legitimate purposes, provided he exercises due care in the selection of the agency and warns the agency that the information must be kept confidential.

This same approach is reflected in Model Rule 1.6, "Confidentiality of Information," which is discussed in **Chapter 3** (*see* section titled "Authorized Disclosure of Confidential Information").

For example, using an outside computerized billing service and a data processing center was deemed appropriate by the California Committee on Professional Responsibility and Conduct. In this opinion, the Committee approved the use of a lawyer's use of an outside data processing center. The Committee also noted that while the practice of law is not a "business," nevertheless, law offices, in accordance with ethical standards, must be allowed to operate as efficiently and economically as possible. Cal. Comm. on Professional Responsibility & Conduct, Formal Op. No. 1971-25 (1971).

3

Understanding the
Requirements for
Confidentiality

WHY CONFIDENTIALITY IS NECESSARY

Confidentiality of client information is arguably the most basic and significant tenet of professional responsibility. The objective is the achievement of complete candor between the client and lawyer, so the lawyer can provide the best representation possible. Ethical Consideration 4-1 of the Model Code provides a clear statement of this requirement:

Both the fiduciary relationship existing between lawyer and client and the proper functioning of the legal system require the preservation by the lawyer of confidences and secrets of one who has employed or sought to employ him. A client must feel free to discuss whatever he wishes with his lawyer and a lawyer must be equally free to obtain information beyond that volunteered by his client. A lawyer should be fully informed of all the facts of the matter he is handling in order for his client to obtain the full advantage of our legal system . . . .

MODEL CODE EC 4-1 (1980).

At the heart of the rules for attorney-client confidentiality is the notion that lawyers are agents of their clients, if not their fiduciaries. Under agency law, agents are prohibited from disclosing or using information confidentially given by the principal (client) or acquired by the agent (attorney) in the course of the agency relationship. The scope of protected information can relate to the client or to the matters in which the agent has been employed. RESTATEMENT (SECOND) OF AGENCY § 395 (1957). *See generally* C. WOLFRAM, MODERN LEGAL ETHICS §§ 6.1, 6.7.1 (1986).

The special nature of the attorney-client relationship, and the rules and ethical considerations governing this relationship, however, expand the responsibility of lawyers to maintain client secrets beyond the standards of agency law. The duty of confidentiality owed by attorneys derives both from the law of agency and the law of evidence.

CONFIDENTIALITY AND ATTORNEY-CLIENT PRIVILEGE

Comparisons of the Different Obligations

The overall duty of confidentiality, although inclusive of the attorney-client privilege, must be distinguished from the nature of the privilege. Confidentiality is given effect in two related bodies of law. The first of these is the attorney-client privilege found in the law of evidence. The rule of confidentiality — established in professional ethics requirements — is based on the law of agency.

The attorney-client **privilege** applies in judicial and other proceedings in which a lawyer may be called as a witness or otherwise required to produce evidence concerning a client. The rule of client-lawyer **confidentiality** applies in situations other than those where evidence is sought from the lawyer through compulsion of law. The confidentiality rule applies not merely to matters communicated in confidence by the client but also to all information relating to the representation, whatever its source.

MODEL RULES Rule 1.6 comment (1983) (emphasis added).

Thus, the attorney-client privilege arises in judicial proceedings, such as trials or depositions when the court seeks direct evidence from the attorney about what the client told the attorney. It also arises when the attorney is requested to produce other evidence regarding the client. Typically, this other evidence protected by the privilege usually falls in the category of "work product." The **work product doctrine** shields from disclosure all memoranda, briefs and other items the attorney has prepared (individually or through others), which relate to the strategy of the case based on the attorney's "mental impressions and thought processes."

While the attorney-client privilege permits the attorney to escape testifying, it must be invoked by the client. On the other hand, either the client **or** the attorney may assert a claim of work-product protection. "The rule . . . that confidential communications by or on behalf of a client may not be disclosed without his consent, has long been a rule of the common law, and is in many jurisdictions the subject of statute. As such, its application is usually a question of law rather than of ethics." H. DRINKER, LEGAL ETHICS 132 (1959).

Continuing Duty to Former and Deceased Clients

The general rule regarding former and deceased clients is that "[t]he duty not to reveal information relating to representation of a client continues after the client-lawyer relationship has terminated." MODEL RULE 1.6(d). Ethical Consideration 4-6 reflects this same obligation: "The obligation of lawyer to preserve the confidences and secrets of his client continues after the termination of his employment . . . ."

Also, Model Rule 1.9, addressing conflict of interest as this issue relates to former clients, states that an attorney may not use information gained **during** the representation of a former client to the disadvantage of that former client, except when permitted by Rule 1.6 or "when the information has become generally known." However, when a former client contacts an attorney **after** representation has ceased and discusses new information with the attorney, the attorney is not obliged to observe the rule of confidentiality with regard to this new information. Because no current attorney-client relationship exists, no duty to protect confidences arises, and the former client will not be able to invoke the attorney-client privilege to protect this new information.

Just as with former clients, the general rule (which requires that attorneys not disclose privileged communications made during the course of representation) continues after the attorney-client relationship has terminated due to the death of the client. The policy behind this rule—that a person seeking the advice of counsel should not fear disclosure of confidential information—is still at work. Knowledge that disclosure may occur after the person's death might stifle the client's need to be candid with the attorney.

AUTHORIZED DISCLOSURE OF CONFIDENTIAL INFORMATION

Should the client reveal confidential communications to a third party or otherwise intend that such communications be revealed, the attorney-client privilege will be considered to be waived. Given the importance of the attorney-client privilege, its loss must be guarded against.

The attorney-client privilege is absolute, with a few critical and very limited exceptions. These exceptions are considered essential for the attorney to function and for the legal system to operate effectively, both in the best interests of the client and the public at large.

When Necessary for Effective Representation

Despite the broad rule of confidentiality, the legal system could not function unless an attorney were permitted to disclose information to employees and independent contractors. Attorneys also need to utilize some confidential information to litigate, negotiate and settle client matters. How, then, do attorneys operate legally and ethically within this ethical rule of confidentiality? The most recent standard states that:

> A lawyer shall not reveal information relating to representation of a client unless the client consents after consultation, **except** for disclosures that are impliedly authorized in order to carry out the representation, ...

MODEL RULES Rule 1.6(a) "Confidentiality of Information" (1983) (emphasis added).

Disclosing information necessary "to carry out the representation" of the client was first discussed in **Chapter 2**, but bears repeating here. It would be impossible to carry out the practice of law without such an exception. The ethical rules recognize this, but also require the attorney to carefully select and train employees. Also, the attorney must supervise nonlawyer employees to ensure that they observe the obligation not to disclose confidential information.

Although the attorney may make disclosures when appropriate for carrying out the representation of a client, the client may still place limits the level of disclosure. By example, lawyers typically discuss client information with other lawyers in their firm. This practice is wholly appropriate unless the client has indicated that the circle of attorneys included in such discussions be limited.

Under the Model Code, the rule of confidentiality is set forth in Canon 4: "A Lawyer Should Preserve the Confidences and Secrets of a Client." "Confidences" and "secrets" are defined as follows:

> "Confidence" refers to information protected by the attorney-client privilege under applicable law, and "secret" refers to other information gained in the professional relationship that the client has requested be held inviolate or the disclosure of which would be embarrassing or would be likely to be detrimental to the client.

MODEL CODE DR 4-101(A) (1980). This presumption of confidentiality, accepted by the majority of states, can only be overcome by the client's consent, or when the attorney deems disclosure necessary in order to represent the client.

Crime-Fraud and Client-Attorney Conflict Exceptions

Model Rule 1.6 outlines additional circumstances when the attorney is permitted to disclose confidential information.

(b) [The] lawyer may reveal such information to the extent the lawyer reasonably believes necessary:

(1) To prevent the client from committing a criminal act that the lawyer believes is likely to result in death or substantial bodily harm or substantial injury to the financial interests or property of another;

(2) To establish a claim or defense on behalf of the lawyer in a controversy between the lawyer and the client, to establish a defense to a criminal charge or civil claim or disciplinary proceeding against the lawyer based upon conduct in which the client was involved, or to respond to allegations in any proceeding concerning the lawyer's representation of the client.

MODEL RULES Rule 1.6(b)(1983).

Under the "crime-fraud" exception, the attorney-client privilege may evaporate when a client consults an attorney in furtherance of a crime or fraud. In some circumstances, the attorney is free to disclose such client communications should an inquiry about the matter be made, and if the conditions of Rule 1.6 are met. Note that this exception permits the attorney to intercede to **only** to prevent the most serious of crimes. Because it is very difficult to know whether a grievous crime will, in fact, be committed, if the attorney chooses not to make any disclosure, in most states, there is no affirmative duty requiring an attorney to disclose this type of information.

What if nonlawyers become privy to information concerning a serious crime? Remember, all employees and independent contractors who work for attorneys are bound by the same rules of confidentiality. In such situations, nonlawyer assistants should tell the attorney about this information, and then ask that attorney to act on it.

Model Rule 1.6 further indicates that an attorney may disclose information in order to defend a legal claim or disciplinary charge brought against the attorney. In the event the attorney is forced to bring a claim against the client to collect unpaid legal fees, for example, confidential information may also be revealed.

HOW TO DISCUSS—<u>WITHOUT</u> DISCLOSING—CONFIDENTIAL INFORMATION

When information becomes public knowledge, as when a lawsuit is filed or a real estate deal is closed, the duty to keep confidential every single piece of information regarding the representation of a client lessens to some extent. In these instances, some disclosures may generally be regarded as permissible and not a violation of the rule of confidentiality. However, since not all information about a representation is ever made public—no matter how illuminating the media spotlight—you must exercise great care in discussing such matters, and limit disclosure only to the facts generally known.

Attorneys and nonlawyers are also frequently confronted with situations where the line between permissible and impermissible disclosures is not clear. In such circumstances, disclosure, if made at all, should be couched in anonymity. That is, the client's name or other identifying information should be withheld. For instance, when "talking shop" with other professionals and support staff, you should discuss any confidential information in a manner that makes it virtually impossible for the listener to identify the client involved. Discussing a case in hypothetical or abstract terms avoids actual disclosure of "information" about a client, and, thus, should not conflict with the language and intent of Model Rule 1.6.

However, if a third party can readily ascertain the identity of the client by virtue of the notoriety of the case or because the client is well known or highly visible, discussion of the matter—even in anonymous or hypothetical terms—is inappropriate. Also, if the attorney or firm is known to specialize in a particular type of practice or client, the same problem exists, because disclosure may also reveal the identity of the client. For example, if the attorney represents only one bank, hospital, celebrity or politician, and that person or entity is known to third parties, then a truly anonymous discussion is impossible, and therefore improper. Of course, in marginal cases, you should **always** err on the side of caution, and not disclose any information at all.

ANALYSIS OF PARTICULAR SITUATIONS

The following discussions flesh out the general rules which apply to common situations involving potential breaches or waivers of confidentiality. While a variety of situations are illuminated, this is by no means an exhaustive list. Particularly as new technologies make inroads into the legal community, and methods of working in law firms change (for example, hiring temporary attorneys), many more opportunities for improperly disclosing confidential information will exist. *See also* discussion in **Chapter 5**, "Common Sense Tips for Protecting Confidential Information."

It is up to every person to guard against disclosing confidential information. As mentioned in the **Introduction**, most breaches of confidentiality are not willful, but even inadvertent disclosure of confidential information can have harmful repercussions.

Inadvertent Destruction of Attorney-Client Privilege

Third party present at conference between attorney and client. One relatively common mistake occurs when the client insists on having a friend, relative or business associate participate in conferences with the attorney. This frequently occurs at the first interview, because the client may need support or simply wants another opinion regarding the suitability of the attorney to handle the particular matter. Circumstances like this could result in the destruction of the attorney-client privilege, because the client is allowing a confidential consultation to be "invaded" by a third party.

Attorneys should resist counseling the client in these situations. If the client persists, the attorney must inform the client of the implications of permitting the presence of a third party. When so advised, the client may still consent to the meeting with a third party present, but knowing that, in all likelihood, this consultation would not be protected by the attorney-client privilege.

Document productions. Some documents requested by opposing parties may contain information subject to the protection of the attorney-client privilege. All documents potentially falling into this category should be inspected by the attorney to determine whether they in fact contain privileged information. Typically, this inspection by the attorney follows the initial review and screening of documents that is performed by either associate attorneys or legal assistants.

Of course, the attorney in charge must supervise this document review task, and provide concrete instructions on identifying potentially privileged documents. The person handling the screening task should err on the side of including even remotely privileged documents. Any potentially privileged documents must be labeled as such and removed from the general document population, pending the attorney's review. *See also* discussion in **Chapter 5**, "Common Sense Tips for Protecting Confidential Information."

Because it can sometimes be quite time-consuming and expensive to review each and every document that is subject to production, the producing party may be tempted to forego such expense and allow the opposing party to inspect all documents. The opposing party may thus be given some documents which would ordinarily be excluded because of attorney-client privilege. If the producing party later wants to assert the privilege, courts will generally find that the privilege had been effectively waived by the producing party's failure to initially review and withdraw any privileged documents. To avoid waiving the privilege inadvertently, all documents potentially subject to production in a litigation matter should be carefully reviewed first.

Confidentiality Requirements Concerning Former Clients

Information relating to a prior matter. A former client contacts an attorney who had worked on a matter for the client at the attorney's former law firm. This former client tells the attorney that the attorney may be required to testify at a trial which involves a client of the new firm (the opponent of the former client). This new communication by the former client to the attorney is **not** subject to the attorney-client privilege, because the professional relationship no longer exists. That is, legal services are no longer being rendered to the former client. Therefore, the attorney is free to notify his new firm that he may be called as a witness in a trial involving one of its present clients.

In this particular case, the attorney was not at all involved in handling or representing the new firm's current client and, in fact, worked in an altogether different department. So there was no direct conflict of interest. On the other hand, the new firm was advised to evaluate whether the potential appearance of the attorney as a witness creates any difficulty or conflict for the firm. N.M. State Bar Advisory Opinions Comm., Op. 1987-4, *construed in* 3 LAWYERS' MANUAL 243 (Aug. 5, 1987).

Nonprofessional contact. After the attorney-client relationship has ceased, a lawyer may learn information from a former client regarding the condition of the former client's business. If a new client approaches the attorney and indicates an interest in purchasing the former client's business, the attorney **may** reveal any damaging information learned from the former client during that "nonprofessional contact," that is, during discussions which occurred outside of the attorney-client relationship.

Continuing Obligations to Deceased Clients

In a case from Massachusetts, a grand jury investigated the possible responsibility of a firm's client for the deaths of two other individuals. The day before the client's death, he consulted with his attorney for two hours in the attorney's office. Although the state wanted the attorney to disclose the substance of the conversation—arguing that the interests of justice override the attorney-client privilege—the court upheld the privilege. Because only the client can waive the privilege, and the client was dead, obviously, there can be no effective waiver. *In re John Doe Grand Jury Investigation*, No. S-5392 (Mass. Sup. Jud. Ct., Nov. 5, 1990), *construed in* 6 LAWYER'S MANUAL 373 (Nov. 21, 1990).

Obligation to Prospective Clients

All prospective clients will convey at least some confidential information to an attorney, even if just about the general nature of the problem for which legal assistance is sought. Because potential clients expect such information to be kept confidential, a confidential situation is created. Thus, the same duty of confidentiality arises even if the attorney declines representation or the prospective client decides not to hire the attorney. Not only does this rule apply when a prospective client verbally consults an attorney, but also applies to any written communications sent to the attorney before the attorney-client relationship is clearly established.

Review of Documents by Unintended Party

It is imperative that any documents sent outside the firm are carefully addressed to the person or entity authorized to receive such documents. This is true whether the documents are mailed, faxed or messengered. If documents are sent to the opposing side in error, or revealed to a third party in violation of the rules concerning confidentiality—even by mistake—not only may the attorney-client privilege be deemed waived, but the client may have an action against the firm for the violation of the ethical rules. For specific guidance on how to avoid making these mistakes, *see* the discussion in **Chapter 5**, "Common Sense Tips for Protecting Confidential Information."

Identity of the Client

The client's name, address and telephone number may be deemed confidential information. Disclosing this type of information could cause the client embarrassment in some circumstances, such as the revelation that someone is a legal services client. ABA Comm. on Ethics and Professional Responsibility, Informal Op. No. 1287 (June 7, 1974).

In more serious scenarios, revelation of a client's identity could engender criminal or civil charges. This was the situation in *Baird v. Koerner*, 279 F.2d 623, 629-30 (9th Cir. 1960). In this case, because the client was making delinquent tax payments, the client's identity was found to be protected by the attorney-client privilege.

Disclosure of Fee Information

Occasionally, clients request that lawyers not disclose their fee arrangements. Such information may fall within the attorney-client privilege, since it is the client who is requesting such confidentiality.

In a criminal case, in which the client sought representation on drug-related charges, the client requested that both his identity and the legal services fee arrangements be kept confidential. When the prosecution sought this information, the court held that since the fee payer was the client and the fee arrangements formed were part of privileged communications, such information does not have to be disclosed. *Caplin & Drysdale Chartered v. United States*, 491 U.S. 617 (1989).

However, in some cases, disclosure of legal fee arrangements, particularly in criminal prosecutions of drug cases, is the subject of some controversy. In federal prosecutions, the confidentiality of the fee arrangement is not guaranteed where there is reason to believe that the money used to pay the fees might have come from illegal activities. Another exception to the general rule which is also applied to criminal cases concerns circumstances where the fee arrangement was not considered part of the subject matter of the professional consultation. *See Tornay v. United States*, 840 F.2d 1424 (9th Cir. 1988); *In re Osterhoudt*, 722 F.2d 591 (9th Cir. 1983).

Consent of the Client

As discussed earlier, upon client consent, attorneys may disclose otherwise confidential information. When the issue of the confidentiality of information is clear, and the client directly consents to disclosure of this information, the matter is easily handled. Other situations, such as those discussed below, are less obvious.

Disclosure of statistical information about firm's practice.
An attorney specializing in wills, trusts and estate planning volunteered as chairman of a charity estate planning committee. The charity requested that the attorney provide statistical, summarized information about the types of legal work he performed in his private practice. Although providing the information to fulfill this request may not appear to present any problems with regard to confidentiality, some risk does exist that confidential client information could be disclosed in these statistics. Clients are entitled to the security of knowing that all confidences conveyed to their attorneys are rigorously maintained, even if individually identifiable information cannot be determined. Los Angeles County Bar Ass'n, Formal Op. No. 403 (Oct. 20, 1982).

"Anonymous" research about clients. A similar situation arose when a nonattorney planned to conduct a research project involving a legal services program. The program was willing to turn over pertinent client information to the researcher, but only if consent from all the clients involved would not be required. (Because of the large number of people from whom consent would have to be solicited, obtaining consent would have been difficult.) Despite the fact that the information sought was to be provided only in summarized form, without listing the names of the legal service's clients, the bar association recommended that protecting the clients' confidentiality should be given the higher priority. Los Angeles County Bar Ass'n, Formal Op. No. 378 (Dec. 12, 1978).

Conflicts Between Clients

The general rule regarding conflicts between existing clients states that an attorney who represents two clients on different matters may not share confidential information with those clients. For example, if an attorney hears information from the first client about the second client, that information may not be disclosed to the second client.

In a specific case from Delaware, a law firm representing two corporate clients was not allowed to reveal to client X the possibility that client Y may file a lawsuit against X. The bar association found that no exception to Model Rule 1.6 applied in this instance. Even though the firm was not representing client Y in connection with the potential lawsuit, it was still bound by the rules of confidentiality.

The bar association determined that Model Rule 1.9 applied in such situations. This Rule states that a lawyer who has represented a client in a matter may not then "use information relating to the representation to the disadvantage of the former client . . . ." Despite the law firm's good intentions in wanting to advise its other client of the possibility of being sued, this type of disclosure is prohibited. Del. State Bar Ass'n Comm. on Professional Ethics, Op. 1990-1 (Jan. 24, 1990), *construed in* 6 LAWYER'S MANUAL 49 (Mar. 14, 1990).

Sharing of Services/Office Space

The problems presented by sharing office space were first discussed in **Chapter 2**, in the context of the level of attorney supervision required. As already mentioned, lawyers frequently lease office space to or from other attorneys or firms. When attorneys also share the services of legal secretaries and a receptionist, maintaining confidentiality of client information can be a definite challenge, as illustrated by the following case from Florida. (*See also* discussion in **Chapter 5**, "Common Sense Tips for Protecting Confidential Information.")

A lawyer shared space with a title company, and the lawyer's files were kept in a common area. This particular office space had some acoustical problems, which permitted others to overhear matters the attorney discussed, although this was possible only when shouting occurred in the attorney's office. When charges were filed against the lawyer, the referee concluded that the attorney had failed to properly secure his files and that the poor acoustical problems would prevent the attorney from preserving client confidentiality.

However, the Florida Supreme Court decided that no violation of the Model Rule 1.6 mandate to keep client information confidential occurred in this situation. The court determined that since no actual disclosure of confidential communications occurred, the attorney had committed no wrongdoing. Also, at the time of the hearing, the attorney no longer shared space with the title company. *Florida Bar v. Wolding*, No. 74,504 (Fla. Sup. Ct. May 9, 1991), *construed in* 7 LAWYERS' MANUAL 153 (June 5, 1991) .

Using Cellular Telephones

Today, cellular telephones, car phones and other mobile communication devices are commonly used by attorneys and others working with attorneys. Frequently, such instruments are used for attorney-client conversations. This use should be avoided as much as possible for two very strong reasons. First, because this form of communication is subject to over-the-air interception, it does not offer a secure forum for exchanging any type of confidential communications. Second, because an expectation of privacy is not reasonable, no attorney-client privilege attaches to such communications.

In a matter squarely presenting the question of whether communications over cellular telephones were privileged, the Illinois State Bar Association concluded that "participants in these conversations have no right to expect to maintain the privacy of their conversation." The bar association noted that a number of courts have held that because mobile telephones are not necessarily private, "individuals using cordless telephones [do] not have a justifiable expectation of privacy . . . even when one end of the conversation was on a land line." As a result, the association also found that confidential communications made over cellular telephones cannot be protected from disclosure by virtue of the attorney-client privilege. Ill. State Bar Ass'n Comm. on Professional Ethics, Op. 90-7 (Nov. 26, 1990).

To guard against losing the protection of the privilege, attorneys (and other professional staff) should always inform the client whenever they place a call from a cellular telephone. This way, both parties can conduct the conversation with the understanding that the conversation cannot be treated as confidential, and thus, the protection afforded by the attorney-client will not be available. *See also* discussion in **Chapter 5**, "Common Sense Tips for Protecting Confidential Information."

4

Conflict of Interest

WHAT CONSTITUTES A CONFLICT OF INTEREST?

The Duty of Loyalty

Underlying the obligation to keep client information confidential is a general "duty of loyalty" to the client. Because attorneys owe their current clients this undivided loyalty, they must avoid any "conflict" which would harm, impair or otherwise negatively impact the "interests" of their clients. Wholly analogous to the rule of confidentiality, the rule against conflict of interest requires attorneys to continually evaluate their obligations to both existing and prospective clients.

This Chapter addresses the avoidance of conflict of interest in light of the attorney's continuing duty to keep client information confidential. Representing adverse (or potentially adverse) client interests necessarily involves weighing whether conflicting confidential communications may occur.

The principles codified in Model Rule 1.7 specify that an attorney may **not** represent a client if that representation would be "materially limited" by his or her responsibilities to another client, to a third party, or because of an attorney's personal interest in a matter. (*See* the **Appendix** for the full text of this Rule.) Note that this obligation to avoid conflicts of interest also applies, in a somewhat limited sense, to former clients. Model Rule 1.9 states that, unless the former client consents, attorneys may **not** represent another client in the same matter, or in a "substantially related" matter, in which the new client's interests are "materially adverse" to the interests of the former client. (*See* the **Appendix** for the full text of Rule 1.9.)

Difficulties in Avoiding Conflict of Interest

Though seemingly logical and simple, real world applications of the conflict of interest principle frequently prove quite difficult. A conflict between the interests of different clients can arise in any number of situations, presenting quite difficult questions about what interests should be protected, and how far a firm must go in protecting the interests at stake. One of the most direct conflicts, of course, would be if an attorney began representing two clients who oppose each other in the same litigation matter. Obviously, such clear conflicts are not allowed. But conflicts of interest can arise in much more subtle ways.

Some troublesome problems can occur when the client is an entity such as a corporation. In such cases, the attorney's primary responsibility is to the corporation, and not the individuals making up the organization, such as the president, chief executive officer or other key management personnel.

Another critical area in which potential conflicts of interest arise is in the employment of legal professionals. Hiring lawyers and legal assistants who were previously associated with opposing law firms or government entities requires checking the depth and extent of involvement by these candidates in matters that are or will be adverse to the firm's current clients. Also, a candidate's personal relationships with other lawyers, judges, law clerks and legal assistants—whether such relationships are with a husband, wife or other immediate family member—must be weighed for any potential conflicts.

For example, say a firm wants to hire an experienced legal assistant who is currently working for a smaller firm. It just so happens that the new firm had opposed the smaller firm in a number of lawsuits. Is the new firm barred from hiring the legal assistant because of her knowledge of these cases? Is the legal assistant limited in her job searches to only those firms against which her old firm had not competed? To what extent, if the new firm hires the legal assistant, must she be shielded from the matters involving her old firm? If such an "ethical wall" is erected, will this be sufficient to successfully oppose a motion to disqualify the new firm on the basis of this potential conflict of interest? (For a more in-depth discussion of this issue, *see* the section titled "Screening Potential Employees for Conflicts of Interest," below.)

Unless the client that is potentially subject to such conflicts consents to continued representation under these circumstances, the law firm must act to avoid the conflict. This may mean having to decline representation of a new client, not becoming involved in a new matter for an existing client or forgoing hiring certain candidates.

EVALUATING CONFLICTS OF INTEREST BETWEEN CLIENTS

Not only are attorneys required to identify all potential conflict problems, but they must also select the appropriate remedial measures. May the attorney implement shielding mechanisms, or is withdrawal and/or disqualification from representation the only solution? This is why having screening mechanisms in place for determining potential conflicts involving new clients is so important. Law firms must also carefully screen all potential hires for possible conflicts with the firm's current clients.

Because proper application of the Model Rules requires weighing a variety of facts and implications, attorneys can only evaluate potential conflicts of interests on a case-by-case basis. Focusing primarily on the conflict between current and potential clients, the firm must analyze the following.

- First, does a potential conflict exist? This involves checking firm records for all parties involved in litigation and transactional matters. This is true not only for named plaintiffs/defendants and other parties on record, but also for any unnamed principals of corporations, for example.

- Second, if confidential information is provided to the attorney, is one client jeopardized by another client presumably having access to this information? What about circumstances where the confidential information may be of little interest to (or already known by) the second client?

- Third, do the clients in conflict require the same or a different type of representation? If there is a conflict, but the matters involving each client are different, i.e., litigation vs. a real estate closing, the conflict may be more easily avoided.

Gaining a client's consent to continued representation may involve the firm agreeing to any of the following modifications to the standard attorney-client relationship.

- If a dispute arises, the lawyer may not represent one client against the other.

- The attorney may not assert a position favorable to one client but disadvantageous to the other client.

- The firm may not represent one client against another client of the firm even in a totally unrelated case.

SCREENING POTENTIAL EMPLOYEES FOR CONFLICTS OF INTEREST

Difficult questions about conflicts must also be considered when lawyers, paralegals and support staff move from one firm to another. Both Model Rule 1.10, "Imputed Disqualification," and Rule 1.11, "Successive Government and Private Employment," apply to the issue of hiring experienced attorneys—and, by extension—legal assistants. Rule 1.10 states:

(a)   While lawyers are associated in a firm, none of them shall knowingly represent a client when any one of them practicing alone would be prohibited from doing so by Rules 1.7, 1.8(c), 1.9 or 2.2.

(b)   When a lawyer becomes associated with a firm, the firm may not knowingly represent a person in the same or a substantially related matter in which that lawyer, or a firm with which the lawyer was associated, had previously represented a client whose interests are materially adverse to that person and about whom the lawyer had acquired information protected by Rules 1.6 and 1.9(b) that is material to the matter.

(c)   When a lawyer has terminated an association with a firm, the firm is not prohibited from thereafter representing a person with interests materially adverse to those of a client represented by the formerly associated lawyer unless:

(1)   the matter is the same or substantially related to that in which the formerly associated lawyer represented the client; and

(2)   any lawyer remaining in the firm has information protected by Rules 1.6 and 1.9(b) that is material to the matter.

(d)   A disqualification prescribed by this Rule may be waived by the affected client under the conditions stated in Rule 1.7.

MODEL RULES Rule 1.10 (1983). *See* the full text of Model Rule 1.11 in the **Appendix**.

Special considerations must be given to hiring situations, particularly in today's climate, because attorneys, paralegals and support staff change employment much more often. A potential employee's working history must be closely evaluated to determine whether any conflicting clients or matters can be found. Any such conflicts must then be analyzed to determine whether they can be overcome.

■ What matters has the person worked on in the past? The new firm obviously needs this information to evaluate potential

conflicts. But, as discussed earlier, revealing the fact that someone was a client of a particular firm might, in some circumstances, be considered disclosing confidential information.

■ What was the level of involvement? It might make a difference
if the person was only marginally involved in a matter at a
previous firm (i.e., a legal secretary who worked on the conflicting matter only when needed for overflow work).

■ How long did the person work at a firm in which a conflicting
matter or client is involved? If only a short period of time is in
issue, and the source of the conflict is not great, there may not
be a problem.

■ Has the person being considered previously participated in any
matter that conflicts with the current clients of the firm?

■ If yes, must the firm withdraw or be disqualified from representation? Or may it effectively "screen" potential employees from
any participation in the questioned matter?

The host of issues just outlined implicate a number of important legal and social considerations, some of which may necessarily
be in conflict. Among these are "a person's right to [the] counsel
of his or her choice, a client's right to confidentiality and loyalty
in his or her relationship with legal counsel, and the right of
attorneys [and legal assistants] to move from job to job." Colo. Bar
Ass'n Ethics Comm., Formal Op. No. 88 (May 18, 1991) (titled "Use
and Misuse of 'Chinese Walls'").

Conflicts of Interest and Nonlawyer Staff

This last issue, "the right to move from job to job," was addressed in a 1990 article that focused particularly the employment
of a paralegal. In this California case, a plaintiff firm with a number
of asbestos cases hired an experienced legal assistant from a defense firm that also handled asbestos cases. In fact, the paralegal
worked on the asbestos cases for his previous employer, and this
experience was one reason he was hired by the plaintiff firm.

The defendant's motion for disqualification of the plaintiff firm
in nine pending asbestos cases was granted because the plaintiff

firm had failed to properly screen the new paralegal from the conflicting cases by creating an "ethical wall:"

> At issue is whether or not attorneys now have a duty to subject paralegals and other support staff to the same rules of conduct that govern attorneys.

> A top California state bar official says yes. "What this says to lawyers is, 'You are now under a duty to screen your paralegals for conflicts in the same way that you screen your associates,'" says Karen Betzner, director of professional competence for the California Bar in San Francisco.

Motamendi, "In California, It's Better to Stay Put than to Switch," *Legal Assistant Today* 37 (May/June 1990). In fact, Betzner went on to say that this same screening rule should probably apply to most experienced support staff, including legal secretaries.

The disqualification order was later upheld by the California appellate court. *In re Complex Asbestos Litigation*, Cal. App. Ct. No. A047921 (July 19, 1991), *construed in* 7 LAWYER'S MANUAL 212 (1991).

The Use of "Ethical Walls"

Sometimes called "Chinese Walls" to denote the complete cutting off of communication about a matter in which a conflict was found, "ethical walls" provide one way for firms to overcome most conflicts. In these situations, the person with the conflict, generally an attorney or legal assistant:

- must be diligently screened from all conversations — especially casual "shop talk" — about the conflicting matter,

- may not be given access to any files or paperwork mentioning or involved in the matter, and

- must also be extremely diligent in avoiding circumstances in which a "breach" of the wall could occur.

Typically, the person with the conflict must also sign an agreement which specifies that he or she will avoid being exposed to any conflicting confidential information.

Of course, the firm must also obtain the client's consent, confirming that creating an ethical wall will be sufficient to guard against shared client confidences.

> An integral part of obtaining the client or former client's informed, written consent is to establish an "ethical barrier" or "cone of silence" to prevent the proposed hire from working on or having access to matters or cases that pose a conflict. . . . The ethical barrier should be established at the outset and a memorandum should be circulated to all attorneys and staff not to communicate with the newly hired employee [or anyone else with a conflict] concerning the subject of the conflict.

Roeca, "Careful Screening Can Avert Conflict Problems," *California Law Business* 30 (Daily Journal Corp., Sept. 16, 1991).

If the client declines to provide written consent to the conflict, the only way for the firm to avoid a motion for disqualification may be to not hire the potential employee who has the conflict. When the conflict is not discovered until after the person has been hired, "the firm may need to terminate his or her employment immediately to avoid a conflict and the appearance of impropriety." *Ibid.*

Special Considerations for Temporary Staff

Law firms and legal departments typically require permanent staff members to sign confidentiality agreements (like the ones found in **Chapter 6** of this monograph). More and more, however, firms are also requiring such agreements from temporary staff. Employers may also conduct comprehensive conflict screening procedures for temporary staff as well, particularly for experienced legal assistants and attorneys.

However, screening a temporary employee's entire working history for potential conflicts can be burdensome. As a result, it often falls upon the agencies representing temporary staff to handle the screening process. Although law firms are required to keep client information confidential, when it comes to hiring temporary employees, the agency involved must have sufficient facts with which to screen for conflicts.

> If a law firm tells the agency the case name and the nature of the work that temporary employees will handle, the agency will be in a better position to screen the placement. It is important to let the agency know the identities of the parties involved in a matter, since a busy agency already may be supplying employees to the opposing side.

Hill, "'Temps' Create Security Issue," *The National Law Journal*, 30 (July 19, 1991).

Of course, if the matter involves litigation and is part of the public record, there are no ethical problems in providing this information to an agency. Difficulties arise, however, if the matter is transactional and the scope of the deal and the number of parties have not yet been identified publicly. In such situations, it is incumbent upon every person working as a temporary employee to volunteer any suspected conflicts as soon as they become apparent.

Confidentiality, Conflict of Interest and Contract Attorneys

Law firms have always used "temporary" employees for overflow work, particularly to handle secretarial or clerical tasks. Hiring legal assistants as temporary staff members is also rather commonplace. It is just in the past few years, however, that the use of temporary attorneys has gained favor in law firms and even in a few corporate legal departments. "'The legal community is having to come to grips with the premise that the traditional ways of doing things require change due to the economy and lifestyle orientations—people want to practice law on their own terms. . . .'" Nance-Nash, "Use of Temporary Lawyers on Rise," *California Law Business*, 27 (Daily Journal Corp., Feb. 24, 1992) (quoting Jess Womack, senior counsel at Atlantic Richfield Co.).

In 1988, the ABA addressed the ethical issues of firms using temporary or "contract" attorneys. In considering this new phenomenon, the opinion first found that temporary attorneys did in fact "represent" clients just as if they were lawyers associated with a firm. As a result, contract attorneys are bound by the same rules as other lawyers. In addition, the ABA found that firms should adopt strict procedures to guard against violation of these ethical requirements.

> [T]o minimize the risk of disqualification, firms should, to the extent practicable, screen each temporary lawyer from all information relating to clients for which the temporary lawyer does no work. All law firms employing temporary lawyers also should maintain a complete and accurate record of all matters on which each temporary lawyer works. A temporary lawyer working with several firms should make every effort to avoid exposure within those firms to any information relating to clients on whose matters the temporary lawyer is not working.

ABA Comm. on Professional Ethics and Professional Responsibility, Formal Op. 88-356 (1988).

Avoiding conflicts of interest while working on a number of matters for different firms can also present a real challenge for temporary attorneys.

> Except for limited circumstances, a contract attorney must not work simultaneously on matters for clients of different firms if the representation of each is materially adverse to the other. Similarly, a contract attorney must not work on a matter for a client of one firm and thereafter work for a client of another firm on substantially the same matter if one client's interest is adverse to the other.

Ors, "Project Attorneys for Temporary Assignments," *Los Angeles Lawyer* 59 (June 1991). Tracking each project, the parties and issues, and the nature or scope of the work involved in each individual assignment means that temporary attorneys face a daunting recordkeeping task that is not currently required of other temporary law firm employees.

ANALYSIS OF PARTICULAR SITUATIONS

The closely associated issues of confidentiality and conflict of interest are confronted in a variety of situations. The most common ones are discussed below.

Representation Adverse to Former Client

The general rule is that attorneys cannot disclose information to a current client which is adverse to a former client. In a Los Angeles case, a law firm withdrew from representing a client after the client revealed that it had intentionally failed to disclose material information on a prospectus filed with the Securities and Exchange Commission, a clear violation of law. When another client of the firm later asked for an evaluation of the first client's financial offering, the firm had a problem. Could—or should—it reveal that the first client had committed securities fraud in connection with that offering?

The bar association ruled that the obligation to keep a client's confidences secret does not end when the representation of the client ends. Unless the firm obtains the consent of the former client to disclose the information, it could not be shared with the second client. Presuming that the first client would not consent to this disclosure, the firm could not effectively represent the second client in evaluating the offering. Since the firm had knowledge of the fraud, yet could not share it, it could only tell the second client that it had a conflict in the matter and decline representation. Los Angeles Bar Ass'n Op. 463 (Oct. 1991), *construed in* 6 LAWYER'S MANUAL 459 (1991).

Changes in Employment

Law firms may be disqualified from representing a client because an attorney or nonlawyer employee was formerly associated with a firm that represented an opposing party. In cases of such direct conflict, the decision regarding disqualification generally turns on whether the attorney or nonlawyer obtained confidential information at the former firm. If an attorney acquired such information, the courts are less reluctant to disqualify the new firm, concluding that it would be quite difficult to guarantee continuing confidentiality. On the other hand, in situations involving a nonlawyer employee, most courts are reluctant to disqualify the employing firm, perhaps on the assumption that the level of confidential information involved might be lower than is the case with attorneys.

Nonlawyer employees. As discussed earlier (in the section titled "Conflicts of Interest and Nonlawyer Staff"), a 1990 case from California ordered a plaintiff law firm disqualified from a number of asbestos cases it handled because of an experienced paralegal the firm had hired. Even though the paralegal had previously worked for firms representing the opposing side of the asbestos litigation, the new firm mistakenly did not erect an ethical wall to prevent sharing of confidential information. As noted in the ABA Lawyer's Manual on Professional Conduct:

> Non-lawyer employees who switch sides in a case aren't held to the same high standards as lawyers who do the same thing, but the law firms that hire them must be careful to screen them from any participation on matters related to those they handled at their former place of employment . . . . [T]he hiring law firm must be disqualified if it can't rebut the presumption that the [confidential] information has been used, by demonstrating either that it obtained a written waiver from the former employer or that it instituted a screening procedure when the employee was hired.

In re Complex Asbestos Litigation, Cal. Ct. App. 1st Dist., No. A047921 (July 19, 1991), *construed in* 7 LAWYER'S MANUAL 212 (July 31, 1991).

The Court of Appeals in this case declined to hold nonlawyer employees to the same standards as attorneys, because to do so would "create unnecessary barriers to employment opportunity." *Ibid.* However, the court also noted that the hiring firm should have instituted a "cone of silence" to screen the paralegal from participation in matters which were involved in the conflict of interest.

From government to private employment. An attorney is not permitted to move from government employment into the private sector and represent anyone connected to a matter where the lawyer participated "personally and substantially" as a public officer. Also, the new law firm with which the lawyer becomes associated is generally barred from undertaking representation which would involve such conflicts unless the government agency consents. The underlying purposes of this rule are:

- to foster the public's confidence in the government,

- to avoid the appearance that the lawyer, while acting as a public official, was (or could be) influenced by the hope of gaining a position in a private concern, and

- to avoid the appearance of public authority being used on behalf of a private client.

Thus, an assistant attorney general who worked on environmental cases concerning certain federal parks, and who later becomes associated with a firm representing other parties to these lawsuits, is precluded from personally participating in these cases. Another lawyer in the firm may avoid being tainted with the same conflict, and thus avoid disqualification, if effective "screening" devices are established.

In a case from California, a former court commissioner who presided over some aspects of divorce cases later joined a private attorney to form a two-lawyer firm. The private attorney represented two clients in cases in which the former commissioner had issued rulings on motions. When the opposing parties sought to disqualify the new firm, the Superior Court noted that even in a two-attorney firm, effective screening of the person with the conflict can overcome a motion for disqualification. As noted in the ABA Lawyer's Manual: "[T]he parties' and the public's perception of impropriety needs to be alleviated by a process that assures that neither the former judge nor his law firm has received or will receive an unfair advantage. Screening serves this purpose." *Higdon v. Superior Court of Kern County*, No. F014568 (Cal. Ct. App., 5th Dist. Mar. 1, 1991), *construed in* 7 LAWYER'S MANUAL 61 (Mar. 27, 1991).

Relatives of Lawyers and Nonlawyers

Generally, lawyers who are relatives may not represent opposing parties. In such situations, the difficulty in maintaining confidentiality and objectivity may be too strained to avoid the appearance of impropriety. A case from Ohio clearly illustrates this rule. In this matter, the prosecutor and the criminal defense lawyer were both siblings and former law partners. In fact, the prosecutor still received income from the former partnership.

The members of the Ohio Board on Grievances and Discipline found that there was indeed a conflict of interest in this situation, noting that Disciplinary Rule 5-101(A) governed. This rule prohibits accepting employment in cases in which the opposing lawyers' professional judgment could be affected by the lawyer's own financial, business, property or personal interests. Ohio Sup. Ct. Bd. of Commissioners on Grievances and Discipline, Op. 91-22 (Oct. 18, 1991), *construed in* 7LAWYER'S MANUAL 372 (Dec. 4, 1991).

In Michigan, a nonprofit legal services organization employed a paralegal who was engaged to marry a farmer. The farmer and his father, also a farmer, were potential defendants in a case handled by the legal services corporation. In fact, the father had been sued by the corporation in the past. The question presented was whether the legal services corporation could employ this paralegal while at the same time proceeding against her future husband and father-in-law on behalf of clients of the organization.

While the State Bar Committee noted that the ABA Model Code did not apply to nonlawyer employees, it found that the same standards must apply, to "ensure that the nonlawyer employees of law firms will not purposely or otherwise aid opponents to the detriment of their employers." Although the consent of the plaintiffs was required first, the bar association found that as long as the legal assistant was barred from access to or involvement in the case, the independence of the attorney handling the case could be preserved. Mich. State Bar Comm. on Professional and Judicial Ethics, Op. CI-1168 (Dec. 10, 1986), *construed in* 3 LAWYER'S MANUAL 10 (Feb. 4, 1987).

5

Common Sense Tips for Protecting Confidential Information

IMPORTANCE OF GOOD WORK HABITS

In addition to following the advice in the examples discussed earlier, the best way to avoid violating confidences is to examine your day-to-day working habits. It is usually through oversight, mistake or simply not paying attention that most violations of confidentiality occur.

Policies should exist that deny unauthorized personnel access to files and to the file room. Code numbers can be used on client files instead of names. Old files and paper (even scratch paper) concerning clients should be disposed of properly so that no one outside the firm will have access to them. Computer screens should not be visible to those walking through the office. Conversations over the intercom and speaker phone should be limited to nonconfidential matters to prevent unauthorized personnel, clients, or others visiting the office from overhearing.

T. CANNON, ETHICS AND PROFESSIONAL RESPONSIBILITY FOR LEGAL ASSISTANTS 99 (1992). Most firms will have already established guidelines and policies for keeping client information confidential. Be sure to read through your firm's employee manual to make sure you understand these particular guidelines.

What follows is a listing of some of the more common situations in which confidences can be inadvertently revealed. Suggested safeguards to avoid disclosure are discussed in turn. While these safeguards should be followed at all times, they are absolutely essential in those instances when confidential information is at risk of being disclosed.

- recognizing that visitors will occasionally be in the firm and in your office

- limiting use of paging systems, speaker phones and intercoms

- using the telephone properly (messages, client information, cellular telephones)

- holding meetings in offices or conference rooms, not in reception lobbies, hallways or other public areas

- talking in face-to-face conversations

- limiting access to files and client documents

- limiting access to information generally to people assigned to matter

- using a limited number of personnel to work on the matter

- clearing desk, office and work space when away from the area

■ blanking computer screens and exiting from system

■ following procedures for computer security systems

■ keeping computer backups and tapes locked up

■ clearing conference rooms of materials and keeping doors closed during meetings

■ marking files or documents "Confidential"

■ protecting original documents with use of working copies

■ keeping photocopy jobs and facsimile transmissions secure

■ using a shredding machine for confidential waste paper

■ determining when security guards are necessary

■ carefully working with outside vendors

■ handling inquiries from the media

THE IMPACT OF VISITORS IN THE FIRM AND IN YOUR OFFICE

At any particular time in a law firm, clients, witnesses, investigators, copy service representatives, equipment repair staff, friends, representatives from the news media, and many other people from outside the firm may be present. These people may be found in the reception area, walking through the halls, in the firm's restrooms, getting a cup of coffee or meeting with others in offices and conference rooms. The mere fact of having such "outsiders" present in the firm presents opportunities for inadvertently disclosing client confidences.

Conversations with clients and conversations relating to confidential client information should only take place in closed offices or conference rooms. **Only the people who need to know** such information should be present at these discussions. **Never** hold such conversations in lunch rooms, reception areas, hallways, elevators or office lobbies.

Not too long ago, a rerun episode of the television show "LA Law," illustrated this situation quite clearly. The actress who plays the entertainment attorney was walking through the secretarial work area and hallways—all public places—while carrying on a lengthy conversation on a cellular telephone. It wasn't clear who was on the other end of the conversation, but from the context of what was said—negotiating over some "deal points"—it could have been the attorney's client, the client's agent or even the head of a movie studio.

If you've read this monograph closely, you've already spotted two key problems. First, this confidential-sounding conversation is taking place over a cellular phone, and courts have already held that there can be no reasonable expectation of privacy in these conversations. Second, the conversation—at least one side of it— was taking place in what was, effectively. a public place. Other clients, temporary staff and even representatives from other studios could have been present. This fictional scene violated one of the key maxims to guard confidentiality: confidential conversations should only take place in areas where confidences can be guarded.

Of course, you can also expect to have occasional visitors to your office. It may be a client or the computer repair person. If you keep your working papers organized, you can easily put away client related, confidential materials before visitors arrive. But when unexpected visitors come in to your office, you also must take care that no confidential information is visibly accessible. By all means, put away confidential materials as soon as you've finished working with them.

Some people tend to stack up the projects they're working on, both to keep them within easy reach and to provide reminders about on-going work. If you prefer this approach, and have stacks of client materials on your desk, you can easily provide some protection by placing these materials in folders to protect them from prying eyes. Because the simple fact that someone is a client of the firm may be considered confidential information, you can label these folders with the firm's client number or other code that you will understand, but others from outside the firm will not.

LIMITING USE OF PAGING SYSTEMS, SPEAKER PHONES AND INTERCOMS

Because clients, service people, witnesses, etc., can be expected to be on the premises of the firm at any time, it is important to remember this fact when using intercoms and paging systems. If the receptionist announces on the firm's office-wide paging system, "Ms. Jones, your client, ABC Bookstore, is on line 2," now everyone in the firm knows that this company is a client of the firm. If your firm specializes in bankruptcy cases, it can be implied that ABC Bookstore is either in bankruptcy now or is contemplating it. Of course, this can have severe consequences for the company.

What the receptionist should do is to announce merely that Ms. Jones has a call waiting on line 2. When Ms. Jones picks up the intercom, then the receptionist can say that it is ABC Bookstore on the line. This way, the goal of announcing the call is accomplished: Ms. Jones is alerted, and client confidences are not revealed.

This same point is true for the use of interoffice intercoms, particularly if the intercom messages are transmitted over the telephone speaker, and not just through the handset. If you're calling another person in the firm on the intercom, and that person just hits the speaker phone button, everything you say will be heard by everyone within earshot of the speaker phone. This could include people passing in the hallway if the person you're calling keeps the office door open.

Therefore, you must be aware of this possibility whenever you use the intercom. If the person you're calling ordinarily uses the speaker phone, or when you can tell that the speaker phone is being used, you **must** limit your conversation to nonconfidential matters. When you need to transmit confidential information, ask the person to pick up the handset.

Another point to always keep in mind is the possibility that the person you're calling may have others in the office. These other people can still overhear at least one side of the conversation, and, in answering your questions or completing the discussion, the person you've called may need to discuss client matters. To avoid the possibility that confidential information will be discussed, the best approach is to simply use the intercom for checking to see if that person is in the office, and to set up a time so you can meet face to face.

TALKING ON THE TELEPHONE

Today's law offices could not function without the use of telephones. Because telephones are an integral part of the day-to-day work of a law firm, everyone must take the appropriate precautions when talking on the phone.

Taking Messages

You may think that this task can't present many opportunities for confidentiality problems. And, in most cases, taking telephone messages is a relatively easy task. However, you must make sure that you do not repeat messages containing confidential information within earshot of others. This applies whether an attorney, paralegal, secretary or receptionist takes the message. Mentioning the nature of the call or specifying the whereabouts of a client or the attorney may result in inadvertent disclosure of confidential information.

For example, the receptionist is constantly taking and relaying messages regarding telephone calls to or from attorneys, legal assistants and other office personnel. Because people from outside the office are frequently waiting in (or passing through) the reception area, they may, as a result, overhear a confidential message. Consider the following possibilities:

- If the receptionist asks a caller for the spelling of a name and then repeats the name back, someone sitting in the waiting room will know who is calling.

- If the receptionist also asks the caller if he or she would care to leave a message, and then repeats that message back to confirm its accuracy, the same problem may occur.

- If the caller asks for someone who is out of the office and the receptionists provides information in detail ("I'm sorry, Mr.

Johnson is at a meeting with ABC Bookstore this morning, would you care to leave a message?"), the receptionist has just told the caller **and** anyone walking through the reception area that ABC Bookstore is a client, and Mr. Johnson is working with that client.

These same potential problems can entangle anyone who answers an outside line. For example, you are standing by a secretary's desk while the secretary is away, and the telephone rings. You answer the telephone and take a message, repeating the information to make sure you get the message correct. If you're standing in the hallway, you may be overheard.

To avoid these problems, you must make sure that you cannot be overheard when you need to repeat information to the caller to confirm accuracy. If this is impossible, then you should not repeat any details which can provide information about clients.

Client Information

Telephone conversations that deal with confidential information should be made **privately**. These conversations must be shielded from possible, even if innocent, listeners. Beware of unanticipated telephone calls — sometimes, the caller needs to impart confidential information, and cannot let you know in advance. In such cases, because you're taken off guard, you may inadvertently repeat part of the conversation and could be overheard if you're not in a secure location. If necessary, put the caller on hold (or simply say that you will call back) while you relocate to a more private setting to continue the conversation.

Be wary of callers asking for information about clients. You should **never** provide client information over the phone unless you are positive that the person calling for this information has been authorized to receive it. If you are unsure at all, obtain the full name, affiliated organization and telephone number for the caller, so you can confirm with the client's attorney whether this person is indeed authorized. You must make absolutely sure that the caller has the right to know the information requested.

Cellular Telephones

The use of cellular and mobile telephones dramatically increases the possibility of being overheard, so you should be on guard when using these types of telephones. It's also a good idea to advise others using mobile or cellular telephones to limit the conversation to nonconfidential information.

Cellular and mobile telephones are particularly popular in Los Angeles (and in other large cities). Almost every attorney has a car phone and frequently, lawyers use portable telephones in the office. A court clerk recently told about a real problem with confidentiality and the use of these phones.

This clerk noted that while attorneys were waiting at the courthouse for docket calls, settlement conferences and the like, many like to keep up with events at their offices. To do so, some attorneys use portable telephones. Much to the clerk's surprise, she has observed attorneys walking around outside a courtroom in crowded corridors carrying on lengthy conversations over these phones, well within earshot of all the other people who are waiting. Some attorneys even use mobile telephones sitting right next to a whole bench full of people. You may sometimes think that no one else could possibly be interested in your conversations, but this is not always true.

HOLDING MEETINGS IN OFFICES OR CONFERENCE ROOMS

Meetings with clients or about client matters should be held in offices or conference rooms, not in reception areas, hallways or other public areas. The doors to the rooms should also be closed, particularly during the initial client conference, during strategy sessions and other times when confidential information is sure to be addressed. Attendance at such meetings should always be limited to those with a need to know the information scheduled for discussion.

Be aware of your meeting room surroundings. Are documents or other materials relating to clients in the space? Is the office or conference room being used as a litigation "war room"? Is the office you've picked for the meeting fairly well soundproofed? Even though you may be meeting in a closed room that is not part of the public space, you cannot necessarily conclude that now you can let your guard down.

Sometimes, you will be meeting with a client at the client's offices. Or you may be meeting with an expert witness, a copy vendor or printer who will be performing work on behalf of a client. You must carry over the same habits outlined above to meetings away from the law firm's premises. Also, you should take only the appropriate client files with you to such meetings, and be sure to take them with you when you leave.

TALKING IN FACE-TO-FACE CONVERSATIONS

When it becomes necessary to discuss confidential matters, do so out of the earshot of others. You should always discuss client matters only with persons who have a "need to know." This rule should be honored both in and out of the office.

Loose talk—by either temporaries or full-time employees—poses perhaps the greatest threat to client confidentiality. After a long day, it is human nature for workers to discuss their jobs with co-workers, friends and family, often in public places. On occasion, an interested party overhears a bit of information that can sway a case.

Hill, "'Temps' Create Security Issues," *The National Law Journal* 30 (July 29, 1991). The best—and most easily followed—rule is to never discuss client matters outside the office.

Pay particular attention to the dangers of holding discussions in the following areas:

■ in the kitchen or coffee area

■ while walking through the hallways

■ in the reception area

■ in elevators, particularly when your firm is only one of several tenants in the building

■ while dining in restaurants, and

■ even in bathrooms, particularly when the firm shares the building's floor space with other tenants.

And, of course, don't forget social situations such as parties, or meetings with co-workers after the work day has ended. Not engaging in these discussions may be especially difficult if your firm has been identified with a "cause celebre," but remember that the sanctions for violating confidences can be severe. The best policy is simply to tell people who ask that you cannot discuss the matter due to ethical considerations.

LIMITING ACCESS TO FILES AND CLIENT DOCUMENTS

Only those persons with a need to know confidential information should be permitted access to client files and records. Particularly confidential files should be stored in a locked file cabinet, room or safe. Access to filing cabinets or to the firm's central file room must be similarly limited.

Some law firms protect confidentiality by using a client code name or number on files or documents. This way, if an unauthorized person does gain access, the information, without the corresponding client code or number, is useless. Most firms have specific guidelines which govern the creation, use and destruction of client files. Be sure you understand these specific policies and follow them carefully.

Because law firms generate so much paper, much of it drafts or duplicate copies, the proper disposal of such paper without violating client confidences can be a challenge. *See* discussion titled "Using a Shredding Machine for Confidential Waste Paper," below.

LIMITING ACCESS GENERALLY TO PEOPLE ASSIGNED TO A MATTER

Whenever possible, it is always a good idea to limit meetings, files, documents and conferences to only those people who have been assigned to work on a matter. Sometimes, of course, this will not be necessary; everyone needs to use the copy center, temporary staff or courier services on occasion. However, as a general approach to keeping confidential matters confidential, limiting the number of people involved to those who will be performing the work is the best policy.

USING LIMITED NUMBER OF PERSONNEL

Attorneys can further protect the confidentiality of a matter by limiting the number of support personnel involved in a matter. For example, if an attorney's secretary is out sick or swamped with work, ordinarily the attorney or paralegal gives the project to another secretary for handling. In such situations, it is far better to use only one or two different secretaries; this will avoid having the scope of project known to a wider circle.

Another example arises in situations requiring the assistance of an outside company or individual. Say the services of an investigator, accountant or other consultant are required. If possible, you should instruct the company or service to limit the number of people on their staffs who will be assigned the project, in order to more easily fulfill the obligation of confidentiality to the firm.

CLEARING WORK SPACE WHEN AWAY FROM AREA

You never know who may stumble by your desk and start peeking at the documents you are in the middle of organizing, drafting, revising or reviewing. For example, it is not uncommon for a legal secretary to work for more than one attorney or paralegal. And at any one time, a secretary may work on a number of matters. As a result, the secretary may have several files and work in progress stacked on his or her desk. It is also not uncommon for an attorney or paralegal to stop by the secretary's desk to drop off new work or check on the status of assignments. If the secretary is away from the desk, the attorney or paralegal may start shuffling through documents and start reading some of the material.

In other frequently occurring situations, people from outside the office may ask to use a telephone if they've just gotten out of a meeting. Or they may stop by to chat. If you're not at your desk, but you've left confidential information in plain sight on your desk, the people who drop in to use the phone or chat could become privy to the information you've left.

Similar scenes can take place in attorneys' offices. A secretary, paralegal, client, office manager, opposing counsel, or friend may also stop by the attorney's office. While waiting for the attorney to return, the visitor may be tempted to start reading the documents left on the desk. Another common scenario occurs when an attorney keeps a number of client files in the office. If someone else needs one of those files, it may be necessary for a member of the support staff to look through all these files to locate one in particular.

All the above examples point to the importance of clearing your desk and office of confidential papers while you are away from your work area. It will also help matters if you keep on your desk (or in your office) only the client files you will need in the foreseeable future. This will limit the amount of material you need to safeguard, and at the same time, forestall other people from coming into your office to look for missing files.

BLANKING COMPUTER SCREENS

In so many circumstances, the use of computers has changed dramatically the ways law firms go about their business. This is true of the individual members and employees of a law firm too. One way computers have changed the practice of law is that now, not only do you need to clear your desk and office of confidential material, you also need to clear your computer screen.

How many times have you been in the middle of drafting a document on the computer and then get interrupted? Sometimes you get a call from your supervising attorney asking you to travel up to the next floor to his or her office. Or you may need to go to the supply room to pick up more legal pads.

Whenever it's necessary to leave the desk, many people simply leave their computers on, leaving the document they were in the middle of drafting there for everyone to see. This opportunity for inadvertently disclosing confidential information parallels the situation of leaving confidential documents on your desk or in your office. Anyone could walk by your computer and see what you were working on. In addition, if your firm employs user identification codes and passwords to protect its computer system, if you leave your computer on while you're in the middle of a document, you've also left the entire system open and unsecured.

Always blank your computer screen when someone from outside the firm stops by your office or desk. And when you need to leave your work area, either turn off your computer or exit out to the user identification and password level.

USING AVAILABLE COMPUTER SECURITY SYSTEMS

Computers and data processing equipment have become so commonplace in the law office that even attorneys have started to use them for more than just paperweights. Because confidential information is most likely being stored in the computer, access to your firm's computer is probably limited by password, user identification code, secured room or another method of physical control.

You should always follow your firm's policies for safeguarding its computer system. This typically means keeping your password confidential or changing it every so often. It also means that you should exit from the system whenever you will be leaving your desk or office.

With the use of modem transmission of data over telephone lines and the expanded use of networked computer systems, additional protection must usually be established to prevent unauthorized persons from gaining access. Sometimes this may take the form of limiting a individual user's capability to "read" (gain access to) certain documents or limiting a user's ability to "write over" (change) other documents. Regardless of the mechanisms used by your firm, realize that it takes everyone following the same rules to keep a computer system secure.

KEEPING COMPUTER BACKUPS AND TAPES LOCKED UP

Computer data files must be backed up periodically, both as a safeguard against a system failure, and to open up space on the computer for additional data. Most firms have detailed computer operation and back-up procedures outlined in their employee handbooks. Depending on the size of the computer systems, some firms use floppy disk back-up systems, while larger computer systems require tape back-ups.

If your firm uses stand-alone computers, you may be the person in charge of backing up your own computer files. If this is the case, you must be sure to back up your files at least once a week (or more often for key documents or matters). And you must keep all computer back-ups in a safe, secure place. (The best approach for comprehensive data back-up is to have one set of back-ups stored on site and another stored away from the firm, but in a secure area, in case of fire, flooding, earthquake or other natural disaster.)

Your firm may also employ computer specialists, technicians, or even a manager of information systems. If so, your responsibility for data back-up will be minimal. However, regardless of the size of the system—whether it is made up of individual computers or a network—you must follow whatever procedures the firm has devised to ensure security.

KEEPING CONFERENCE ROOMS CLEARED OF MATERIALS

A number of firms must use at least a few of their conference rooms for managing litigation cases. Such "war rooms" are used for strategy sessions and to house discovery document libraries. As a result, the number of conference rooms that are available solely for meetings is sometimes in short supply. This means that all conference rooms must be checked ahead of time to clear them of any client materials and documents. This is particularly important for scheduled meetings at which people from outside the firm will be in attendance. Firms frequently schedule meetings with opposing counsel and clients for conference rooms, especially when a large number of people will be in attendance.

In checking the conference room, you may find that the conference room contains client materials. If the room contains something like 50 boxes, all marked with a clearly identifying legend like "ABC Bookstore Bankruptcy," you should try to reschedule the meeting to another conference room. If this is not possible, all client materials should be removed or at least camouflaged, so that all client information—and that means even the identification of a client—is not apparent to the meeting attendees.

Once you've checked and cleared the conference room, be sure that the doors are kept closed while the meeting is in session. And, of course, all documents brought to or used during the meeting should be removed from the conference room after the meeting ends.

For example, before a deposition, the attorney or paralegal ordinarily meets with the client, and may bring files in for review. Take care not to leave client files on the conference table after the client meeting, because after the first meeting has ended, the receptionist may show the opposing counsel into the same conference room to begin the deposition.

Sometimes, legal assistants and attorneys require a conference room in which to work on specific projects. For example, a legal assistant might need a large amount of table space on which to organize documents. An attorney may need a quiet room, away from the busy telephone, in which to draft a brief. The documents needed for these projects may be left in the conference room while the attorney or paralegal goes to lunch, attends a meeting or leaves for the day. This means that confidential information could inadvertently be disclosed to unauthorized persons.

If you require the use of a conference room, you should secure the right to use the room exclusively and keep the door locked when the conference room is not in use. Of course, file away all documents in the appropriate folders and filing cabinets once the project is completed.

MARKING FILES OR DOCUMENTS "CONFIDENTIAL"

It never hurts to stamp all client files and work product documents with a big red "confidential" stamp, although there is no guarantee that even documents marked "confidential" will, in fact, be kept confidential. There are some benefits to this approach, however:

- A bright red "confidential" stamp does act as a reminder to treat documents carefully.

- Seeing documents stamped "confidential" puts third parties on notice that this information is not intended for their consumption.

- A "confidential" stamp may expedite the return of loose or "stray" files or documents.

But even if you're working only with documents stamped with this legend, you must still follow the basic rules for dealing with and protecting all client documents.

A representative for an outside copy service recently told the following story. It seems that a messenger was returning 10 boxes of original documents and a corresponding number of boxes of copied documents to a law firm located in a high-rise building. For some reason, the messenger couldn't get the elevator door to stay open while he delivered the first set of boxes back to the law firm client. So, he used a box—one that happened to be marked "confidential" on the lid and sides—to prop open the elevator doors while he made the first of several deliveries.

Unfortunately, the "confidential" box slipped back into the elevator cab, and the door closed. Naturally, this elevator, freed from its constraints, responded to buzzers on other floors. For about an hour, the elevator with several boxes of documents, including one marked "confidential," rode up and down the 20-story building before the hapless messenger could finally catch it again. The documents in the "confidential" box were checked and everything appeared to be in order. But you can be sure that that particular copy service will never hear from the client law firm again. (It is not known if anything happened to the person in the firm who suggested using this copy service in the first place.)

PROTECTING ORIGINAL DOCUMENTS

All original client documents should be kept in file folders in filing cabinets, with working copies made available. Everyone involved in the matter should avoid using the original documents for discussion, drafting or copying purposes (after the first copy set has been created). It is just too easy to spill food or beverages, accidentally mark documents or otherwise mar them.

Even though the documents you may work with on a day-to-day basis are just copies, this does not mean that they should not be protected. Copied documents still contain confidential information, and even inadvertently disclosing this information by not securing your working files is a violation of the ethical rules regarding confidentiality.

When you are through with your working copies, you should take care to dispose of them according to your firm's policies. It may be that all waste paper must be shredded. Or the firm may purge its working files periodically and incinerate all old files at once. Whatever the policy, as long as you have copies of confidential documents you must keep them secure. (*See* discussion below, "Using a Shredding Machine for Confidential Waste Paper.")

SECURING PHOTOCOPYING JOBS AND FACSIMILE TRANSMISSIONS

Take care to not leave behind any documents, confidential or otherwise, on the photocopy machine. Likewise, be sure to collect all documents from the facsimile (fax) machine once transmission is completed. Of course, when working with confidential documents, you (or your secretary) should not leave either the photocopy or fax machine unattended.

When sending a facsimile transmission, be sure to double-check the material to be sent, and confirm that you have the correct fax number. You don't want to send top-secret jury profiles to the opposing party by accident. If faxing confidential material, first advise the intended recipient that you will be sending a confidential fax, to ensure that he or she is available and can be waiting to pick it up.

Always use a facsimile cover sheet that specifies the addressee and the correct fax number. This cover sheet should also contain instructions which advise any unintended recipients that the document being faxed is privileged and should be returned immediately if received by anyone other than the person to whom it is addressed.

USING A SHREDDING MACHINE FOR CONFIDENTIAL WASTE PAPER

As pointed out above, when discussing the importance of limiting access to files and how to protect original documents, it is very important to properly dispose of duplicated client documents, draft documents which deal with client matters, and even all those discarded files and memoranda. One method some firms have adopted is to make available shredding machines for staff use.

Those firms utilizing shredding machines should have established policies for when and if certain documents should be shredded. Sometimes, this is decided on a client-by-client basis. In other circumstances, the firm may simply choose to shred specific document types. Regardless of the particular system at use in your firm, be sure to consider the following situations.

Always check with the supervising attorney before shredding any document. It may be that this is the last copy of a particular corporate document, and even though it is quite old, it still has utility. Be aware, however, that some people working in the legal profession are known pack rats, and will never okay the shredding of documents.

One particularly good example of when documents should be destroyed is multiple copies of a very confidential document. Because the more copies of a document you have, the greater likelihood that confidentiality can be breached, all excess copies of confidential documents should be shredded.

Other circumstances may warrant document shredding or disposal. It could be that more current information or documentation has been obtained. If so, it might be better to destroy all now-outdated documents in order to lessen the likelihood of confusion.

However, always make certain that documents (and other information, such as computer files), which might be subject to discovery are not inadvertently or purposely destroyed. Similar careful considerations should be weighed before destroying cassette tapes, videotapes or other electronically recorded information: e.g., a videotaped will, a taped conversation, videotaped deposition.

DETERMINING WHEN SECURITY GUARDS ARE NECESSARY

In the rare event that information needs to be highly restricted, and fear exists that such information may be tampered with, the retention of security guards may be appropriate. Such restrictions may also be imposed on behalf of a particularly cautious client.

In these cases, the rules described in this monograph are even more important. Complete security may be so important that it becomes necessary to issue "passes" to authorized people. This type of situation would certainly foreclose using any outside services, unless similarly strict security measures could be guaranteed.

CAREFULLY WORKING WITH OUTSIDE VENDORS

As described in the example of the "confidential" box going on the elevator ride (*see* "Marking Files of Documents 'Confidential'"), you can never be absolutely sure what will happen with client documents when an outside service or vendor becomes involved. At a minimum, you should only work with vendors who have already signed confidentiality agreements with your firm and whose work is known and trusted.

Naturally, ensuring security in the use of off-site services must be a top priority. Law firms need to question their service suppliers to ensure that the office where sensitive documents will be storied and processed is secured and not easily accessible to outside traffic.

Some services [particularly deposition summarizing services] allow their personnel to take work home, . . . but this increases the likelihood of a breach. Ideally, the processing area should be located apart from highly trafficked areas and should not be readily identifiable by signs in the lobby or on the office door. . . . The more people who come into contact with a document, the greater the security risk.

Hill, "'Temps' Create Security Issues," *The National Law Journal* 30 (July 29, 1991).

HANDLING INQUIRIES FROM THE MEDIA

You should **never** respond to media inquiries without first seeking the direction of the managing attorney, the firm's administrator (or office manager), or your supervising attorney. Instead, you should tell the reporter that you will refer this call or question to the appropriate person. If your firm's guidelines permit, you may also tell the reporter that someone will return the call later with the appropriate information.

Pending Matters

Occasionally, your office may become involved in a matter which is of some notoriety. The client may be well known or the case may be of particular public interest, or it may feature unique facts or legal theories. A recent example of this type of case is the William Kennedy Smith criminal trial.

As a result, members of the media may call the firm or appear at the office door seeking stories or responses to questions. The reporter may simply be looking for background information or may really want more dramatic statements. In either event, the attorney handling the matter or the managing partner are the appropriate persons to make any statements.

Even if you have all the necessary information with which to provide a response, you always run the risk of disclosing inappropriate information. You may also inadvertently cast the case, client or even the firm in a harmful light. Remember, once confidential information is disclosed, it can never be retracted.

Protection of the client's interests is your firm's primary objective. The attorney and the client must decide whether statements should be made to the media at all. And the attorney must also consider whether giving statements may help or jeopardize the quality of the legal representation.

Your firm may not be involved in handling a high profile matter, but the firm may handle the affairs of a public figure's spouse, business partner or corporation. Here again, no information should be disclosed without attorney direction. So even if representatives from "60 Minutes" show up at your door, you will have to refer them to the designated spokesperson for the firm.

Firm Operations

You may also receive inquiries about the management or members of the firm. This has been an especially hot topic in the last two or three years, as the national economic recession has hit law firms like never before. You may think that responding to these questions cannot possibly involve matters of client confidentiality.

Wrong. Even responding to questions regarding whether certain partners are leaving the firm can reveal information about clients. It may also interfere with ongoing client relationships. Again, a supervising or managing attorney should respond to such questions.

In larger firms, there may be a committee or spokesperson specially designated to advise on the appropriateness of the media's request. Such a committee may also be designated to respond to any and all media queries. You should determine who is the responsible person or committee in your firm, and familiarize yourself with any other firm guidelines regarding media contacts.

6

Model Policy Statements and Employee Guidelines Concerning Confidentiality

SAMPLE POLICY STATEMENT/ACKNOWLEDGEMENT NUMBER 1

_____

(Name of Firm)

Confidentiality Agreement

In consideration of my association with _____ (hereinafter the "Firm"), whether as a partner, associate, "of counsel,"
employee, independent contractor, or otherwise affiliated, the undersigned acknowledges the following restrictions and agrees to
abide to each and every restriction:

(1) Attorneys are charged with the responsibility to preserve the
confidences of their clients. In the normal operation of this
office, I will be exposed to confidential client information. I
understand that this obligates the Firm to carefully select and
train employees and others to ensure that all persons working
within the office, or at the direction of an attorney, also respect
this duty of confidentiality.

(2) I acknowledge the duty and obligation that I have to protect the
confidences of the Firm's clients.

(3) No attorney, employee, independent contractor, or other person
affiliated with the Firm is permitted to purchase, sell or
otherwise trade in the property, stock or other securities of any
corporation, partnership or other entity or individual which the
Firm represents without the prior written consent of a Partner of
the Firm.

(4) No attorney, employee, independent contractor, or other person
affiliated with the Firm shall purchase, sell or otherwise trade in
the securities of any company with which the Firm is involved,
when such purchases are based upon nonpublic knowledge or
information which may be gained while working for the Firm or
while in its offices. I acknowledge that civil and/or criminal
liability may attach for trading on such nonpublic, material
"inside" information.

_____

(Signature)   (Date)

_____

(Name — Please Print)

SAMPLE POLICY STATEMENT/ACKNOWLEDGEMENT NUMBER 2

_____

(Name of Firm)

Confidentiality Agreement

In consideration of my association with _____ (here-inafter the "Firm"), whether as a partner, associate, "of counsel," employee, independent contractor, or otherwise, the undersigned acknowledges the primary goal of the Firm is to provide its clients with the best legal representation possible, and to that end, the undersigned agrees to abide by the following restrictions:

(1) Attorneys are charged with the responsibility to preserve the confidences of their clients. In the normal operation of this office, I will be exposed to confidential client information. This obligates the Firm to carefully select and train employees or others in order to ensure that all persons working within the office or at the direction of an attorney also respect this duty of confidentiality.

(2) No attorney, employee, independent contractor, or other person affiliated with the Firm is permitted to purchase, sell or otherwise trade in the stock or other securities of any corporation, partnership or other entity which the Firm represents without the prior written consent of a Partner of the Firm.

(3) No attorney, employee, independent contractor, or other person affiliated with the Firm shall purchase, sell or otherwise trade in the securities of any company with which the Firm is involved based upon nonpublic knowledge or information which he or she may gain while working for the Firm or while in its offices. There is civil and/or criminal liability for trading on nonpublic, material "inside" information.

(4) Attorneys are generally not permitted to practice law in partnership with anyone but other licensed attorneys, and the employment, services or property sought from the under-

signed do not constitute the forming of any partnership or interest in a partnership, law corporation or otherwise.

(5) In conjunction with (4) above, any salary, wages or other compensation tendered to the undersigned shall not be construed as the sharing of legal fees, except to the extent the Firm may include the undersigned, if at all, in a compensation or retirement plan.

_____

(Signature)   (Date)

_____

(Name—Please Print)

MODEL EMPLOYEE GUIDELINES

Confidentiality Rules to Live By

- Always Respect the Confidentiality of Clients

- Take All Necessary Steps to Protect Documents or Physical Evidence in Your Possession or Under Your Supervision

- Do Not Discuss Confidential Client Information with Other Employees or Third Parties Not Involved in a Particular Matter ("Third Parties" includes family, friends and colleagues)

- Do Not Use Confidential Information to the Detriment or Disadvantage of a Client

- Be Sure Your Participation in a Matter Does Not Conflict with the Firm/Attorney/Business Where You Are Employed or with Whom You Are Associated

- If in a Supervisory Position, Make Certain that Employees and Independent Contractors Have Been Given Adequate "Ethical" Training

- **When in Doubt, Always Err on the Side of Caution**

Guidance for Accepting New Assignments

Always clarify the following facts and issues when first meeting with an attorney about a new assignment:

- What type of matter is it?

- What is your expected level of participation?

- What aspects of matter are you responsible for researching, drafting or completing?

- To what extent must you discuss this matter with others? Is discussion appropriate?

- Inquire whether any special confidentiality problems exist. If so, does the supervising attorney have particular rules or guidelines that you must follow?

Appendix

ABA MODEL RULE 1.2

Scope of Representation

(a) A lawyer shall abide by a client's decisions concerning the objectives of representation, subject to paragraphs (c), (d) and (e), and shall consult with the client as to the means by which they are to be pursued. A lawyer shall abide by a client's decision whether to accept an offer of settlement of a matter. In a criminal case, the lawyer shall abide by the client's decision, after consultation with the lawyer, as to a plea to be entered, whether to waive a jury trial and whether the client will testify.

(b) A lawyer's representation of a client, including representation by appointment, does not constitute an endorsement of the client's political, economic, social or moral views or activities.

(c) A lawyer may limit the objectives of the representation if the client consents after consultation.

(d) A lawyer shall not counsel a client to engage, or assist a client, in conduct that the lawyer knows is criminal or fraudulent, but a lawyer may discuss the legal consequences of any proposed course of conduct with a client and may counsel or assist a client to make a good faith effort to determine the validity, scope, meaning or application of the law.

(e) When a lawyer knows that a client expects assistance not permitted by the rules of professional conduct or other law, the lawyer shall consult with the client regarding the relevant limitations on the lawyer's conduct.

ABA MODEL RULE 1.6

Confidentiality of Information

(a)   A lawyer shall not reveal information relating to representation of a client unless the client consents after consultation, except for disclosures that are impliedly authorized in order to carry out the representation, and except as stated in paragraph (b).

(b)   A lawyer may reveal such information to the extent the lawyer reasonably believes necessary:

> (1)   to prevent the client from committing a criminal act that the lawyer believes is likely to result in imminent death or substantial bodily harm; or

> (2)   to establish a claim or defense on behalf of the lawyer in a controversy between the lawyer and the client, to establish a defense to a criminal charge or civil claim against the lawyer based upon conduct in which the client was involved, or to respond to allegations in any proceeding concerning the lawyer's representation of the client.

ABA MODEL RULE 1.7

Conflict of Interest

General Rule

(a)   A lawyer shall not represent a client if the representation of that client will be directly adverse to another client, unless:

> (1) the lawyer reasonably believes the representation will not adversely affect the relationship with the other client; and

> (2) each client consents after consultation.

(b)   A lawyer shall not represent a client if the representation of that client may be materially limited by the lawyer's responsibilities to another client or to a third person, or by the lawyer's own interests, unless:

(1) the lawyer reasonably believes the representation will not be adversely affected; and

(2) the client consents after consultation. When representation of multiple clients in a single matter is undertaken, the consultation shall include explanation of the implications of the common representation and the advantages and risks involved.

ABA MODEL RULE 1.8

Conflict of Interest

Prohibited Transactions (relevant sections only)

(b) A lawyer shall not use information relating to representation of a client to the disadvantage of the client unless the client consents after consultation...

(i) A lawyer related to another lawyer as parent, child, sibling or spouse shall not represent a client in a representation directly adverse to a person who the lawyer knows is represented by the other lawyer except upon consent by the client after consultation regarding the relationship.

ABA MODEL RULE 1.9

Conflict of Interest

Former Client

A lawyer who has formerly represented a client in a matter shall not thereafter:

(a) represent another person in the same or a substantially related matter in which that person's interests are materially adverse to the interests of the former client unless the former client consents after consultation ; or

(b) use information relating to the representation to the disadvantage of the former client except as Rule 1.6 would permit with respect to a client or when the information has become generally known.

ABA MODEL RULE 1.10

Imputed Disqualification

General Rule

(a) While lawyers are associated in a firm, none of them shall knowingly represent a client when any one of them practicing alone would be prohibited from doing so by Rules 1.7, 1.8(c), 1.9 or 2.2.

(b) When a lawyer becomes associated with a firm, the firm may not knowingly represent a person in the same or a substantially related matter in which that lawyer, or a firm with which the lawyer was associated, had previously represented a client whose interests are materially adverse to that person and about whom the lawyer had acquired information protected by Rules 1.6 and 1.9(b) that is material to the matter.

(c) When a lawyer has terminated an association with a firm, the firm is not prohibited from thereafter representing a person with interests materially adverse to those of a client represented by the formerly associated lawyer unless:

(1) the matter is the same or substantially related to that in which the formerly associated lawyer represented the client; and

(2) any lawyer remaining in the firm has information protected by Rules 1.6 and 1.9(b) that is material to the matter.

(d) A disqualification prescribed by this Rule may be waived by the affected client under the conditions stated in Rule 1.7.

ABA MODEL RULE 1.11

Successive Government and Private Employment

(a)   Except as law may otherwise expressly permit, a lawyer shall not represent a private client in connection with a matter in which the lawyer participated personally and substantially as a public officer or employee, unless the appropriate government agency consents after consultation. No lawyer in the firm with which that lawyer is associated may knowingly undertake or continue representation in such matter unless:

(1)   the disqualified lawyer is screened from any participation in the matter and is apportioned no part of the fee therefrom; and

(2)   written notice is promptly given to the appropriate government agency to enable it to ascertain compliance with the provisions of this rule.

(b)   Except as law may otherwise expressly permit, a lawyer having information that the lawyer knows is confidential government information about a person acquired when the lawyer was a public officer or employee, may not represent a private client whose interests are adverse to that person in a matter in which the information could be used to the material disadvantage of that person. A firm with which that lawyer is associated may undertake or continue representation in the matter only if the disqualified lawyer is screened from any participation in the matter and is apportioned no part of the fee therefrom.

(c)   Except as law may otherwise expressly permit, a lawyer serving as a public officer or employee shall not:

(1)   participate in a matter in which the lawyer participated personally and substantially while in private practice or nongovernmental employment, unless under applicable law no one is, or by lawful delegation may be, authorized to act in the lawyer's stead in the matter; or

(2)   negotiate for private employment with any person who is involved as a party or as attorney for a party in a matter in which the lawyer is participating personally and substantially.

(d)   As used in this Rule, the term "matter" includes:

(1) any judicial or other proceeding, application, request for a ruling or other determination, contract, claim, controversy, investigation, charge, accusation, arrest or other particular matter involving a specific party or parties; and

(2) any other matter covered by the conflict of interest rules of the appropriate government agency.

(e) As used in this Rule, the term "confidential government information" means information which has been obtained under governmental authority and which, at the time this Rule is applied, the government is prohibited by law from disclosing to the public or has a legal privilege not to disclose, and which is not otherwise available to the public.

ABA MODEL RULE 5.1

Responsibilities of a Partner or Supervisory Lawyer

(a) A partner in a law firm shall make reasonable efforts to ensure that the firm has in effect measures giving reasonable assurance that all lawyers in the firm conform to the rules of professional conduct.

(b) A lawyer having direct supervisory authority over another lawyer shall make reasonable efforts to ensure that the other lawyer conforms to the rules of professional conduct.

(c) A lawyer shall be responsible for another lawyer's violation of the rules of professional conduct if:

(1) The lawyer orders or, with knowledge of the specific conduct, ratifies the conduct involved; or

(2) The lawyer is a partner in the law firm in which the other lawyer practices, or has direct supervisory authority over the other lawyer, and knows of the conduct at a time when its consequences can be avoided or mitigated but fails to take reasonable remedial action.

ABA MODEL RULE 5.2

Responsibilities of a Subordinate Lawyer

(a) A lawyer is bound by the rules of professional conduct notwithstanding that the lawyer acted at the direction of another person.

(b) A subordinate lawyer does not violate the rules of professional conduct if that lawyer acts in accordance with a supervisory lawyer's reasonable resolution of an arguable question of professional duty.

ABA MODEL RULE 5.3

Responsibilities Regarding Nonlawyer Assistants

With respect to a nonlawyer employed or retained by or associated with a lawyer:

(a) A partner in a law firm shall make reasonable efforts to ensure that the firm has in effect measures giving reasonable assurance that the person's conduct is compatible with the professional obligations of the lawyer;

(b) A lawyer having direct supervisory authority over the nonlawyer shall make reasonable efforts to ensure that the person's conduct is compatible with the professional obligations of the lawyer; and

(c) A lawyer shall be responsible for conduct of such a person that would be a violation of the rules of professional conduct if engaged in by a lawyer if;

(1) The lawyer orders or, with the knowledge of the specific conduct, ratifies the conduct involved; or

(2) The lawyer is a partner in the law firm in which the person is employed, or has direct supervisory authority over the person, and knows of the conduct at a time when its consequences can be avoided or mitigated but fails to take reasonable remedial action.

ABA MODEL RULE 5.5

Unauthorized Practice of Law

A lawyer shall not:

(a) practice law in a jurisdiction where doing so violates the regulation of the legal profession in that jurisdiction; or

(b) assist a person who is not a member of the bar in the performance of activity that constitutes the unauthorized practice of law.

ABA MODEL RULE 8.4

Misconduct

It is professional misconduct for a lawyer to:

(a) violate or attempt to violate the rules of professional conduct, knowingly assist or induce another to do so, or do so through the acts of another;

(b) commit a criminal act that reflects adversely on the lawyer's honesty, trustworthiness or fitness as a lawyer in other respects;

(c) engage in conduct involving dishonesty, fraud, deceit or misrepresentation;

(d) engage in conduct that is prejudicial to the administration of justice;

(e) state or imply an ability to influence improperly a government agency or official; or

(f) knowingly assist a judge or judicial officer in conduct that is a violation of applicable rules of judicial conduct or other law.

UNWRITTEN RULES **INDEX**

COUNTING THE MINUTES INDEX

CONFIDENTIALITY **INDEX**